the
Worm
Turns

by

Stormy

Pageant Press   New York

First Edition

MANUFACTURED IN THE UNITED STATES OF AMERICA BY
BOOK CRAFTSMEN ASSOCIATES

TO
E. B. and C. B.
Who Made My Dreams Come True

THE WORM TURNS

Chapter 1

SARAH CAME IN FROM THE GARDEN, A LITTLE OUT OF BREATH FROM stooping, brushing the fresh, wet dirt from her knees. She pushed back a strand of hair with a dirty hand and left a smudge on her face. The grocery boy was coming out of the kitchen door when she reached the back porch.

"Hi, Mrs. Davis! I put your things on the table."

"Wait a minute, Joe; don't go without some of my fresh cookies!"

He stood, grinning and willing, in the doorway while Sarah went to the cookie jar. She remembered her hands just in time.

"Here, come and get them, or you'll be eating my garden dirt, too."

With a hasty thanks he was gone, and Sarah smiled after him, thinking how much all young people were alike—her own Helen had much the same ways and manners as young Joe.

George wouldn't like her to say that. To him, the sun rose and set on Helen. That might be a trite saying, but it was certainly a true one. No other teen-ager could possibly be compared with his daughter.

Sarah looked over the enormous box of groceries, and sighed a little. "Well, there's no time like the present."

She began sorting out the canned vegetables and fruits, stack-

1

ing them in their respective rows on the pantry shelf. A car stopped in the driveway. She moved to the window and watched her husband signal to another car at the curb; probably a brother salesman. Her eyes followed the two men up the walk. George was laughing and gesticulating as he led the way to the front door. "Bragging about his yard, that I take care of," Sarah thought without bitterness. "How he likes to take the credit!"

She glanced down at her damp and grimy dress, and thought, "Better not show myself to George's friend."

She heard George saying, in the front hall, "Make yourself comfortable, Red, while I hang up my coat." Sarah heard him moving around and then he called her, "Sarah, you home?"

She moved farther into the pantry and did not answer.

"I guess my wife is out gabbing somewhere—well, we'll have a little drink, Red. It'll warm us up." The faint clink of glasses reached her ears.

The man, Red, had the booming, too-jovial voice of some professional salesmen. "What are you doing this Friday night, George?"

It was hard to hear George's answer, something about traveling so much that he just stayed put when he got home.

Then the booming voice carried clearly to Sarah again. "The H.B.O.S. Club is going to have a big shindig, and we need a guest speaker. I can't think of one better than you, especially when it concerns salesmen. We want an extemporaneous talk, light and amusing chatter, about the salesman in the field."

George's voice answered.

Then: "Oh, everybody will probably be three sheets in the wind, anyway, so just think up something funny to say. Don't worry about it."

Footsteps sounded in the front hall again. Sarah came out of hiding into the gleaming kitchen.

"Oh, I forgot, you can bring somebody if you want to, wife, or girl friend."

Sarah stopped short with her hand on the empty grocery carton.

2

"Sarah go to a wild party like that?" George's voice carried clearly now. "She's not the type. She'd rather work in her rose garden than have dinner at the Marine Dining Room." An amused chuckle reached Sarah's ears.

"Never mind, George, I've got a slick chick on my list I'll put next to you."

"That will be better, Red."

From the kitchen window Sarah watched George walk Red to his car. Suddenly there were tears in her eyes, threatening to overflow. "No, I'm not the type, not in twenty years."

She dabbed at her eyes and slipped out the door, and made her way through the garage into the back yard. Five minutes later she re-entered the house. "George, are you here?"

"Yes, dear, I'm in the bedroom." George stopped in his tracks as he caught a glimpse of his wife's disheveled appearance. "Digging again?" He bent and kissed her on the forehead.

"I've been transplanting bulbs all day. I'll wash up and get dinner started."

"Where's Helen?" That was always in the front of George's mind: "Where's Helen?" The apple of his eye; but Sarah could not criticize him for that, for Helen was very nearly her own excuse for living.

"She went to the library, George."

George settled himself in his favorite chair and smiled as he pictured his daughter doing research work among all the big books in the library. She was definitely not a book worm. She reminded him of an elf, dancing on the sunbeams; cute as a button, and as fresh as the lake breeze, so different from Sarah. Sarah was a good wife, a wonderful mother, the best cook in the world and such a calm, sensible person to be around. Just a little brown wren. But Helen—no, she wasn't an elf, she was a humming bird, quick, small and full of delightful noises and music. She didn't talk, she sang; she didn't walk, she danced; the piano jumped to jive and boogie woogie when she was around. The only time she was quiet was when she took time out to sleep. And she was pretty adult for her sixteen years, too.

3

"What a girl, what a girl!" George sighed contentedly, and stretched out full length. He was getting just a bit thick around the middle. He patted it briefly, "Ought to go on a diet, before it gets too bad," he thought as he closed his eyes and drifted off into a cat nap.

Sarah came out of the bathroom, clean and neat. She stood quietly, observing her husband as he slept. "Too much pastry; too many second helpings." She smiled as she recognized her thoughts. George wouldn't like them. How thin his hair was getting on the top. It used to be so black and thick, but it was even faded now. His face was a bit red, too. Poor George, he wasn't the best looking husband a wife could have, but he was good, kind, an indulgent father, a good provider and a nice man . . . Better than some women got.

There was only one thing that hurt . . . he didn't try to understand her. He had never asked her to share any of the social life he indulged in. That hurt more than anyone could possibly guess. Was it that he didn't want her with him, or was it that he just didn't give it a thought? How did he know whether she was the type or not?

She wandered over to the mirror above the buffet, and looked at her own familiar face closely. Maybe George was ashamed of her. Mousy brown hair, cut rather short, with a fringe of bangs over her forehead. She had worn her hair that way for so many years, she couldn't remember looking any different. Just once she had her hair curled tight and pushed back of her ears, but George had made so much fun of her protruding ears that never again would she expose them.

She had a slight hump in the middle of her nose, broken when she was a child. The tip was a little large; it looked more like a lump. Her fingers traced her eyebrows, too thick and heavy. Soft blue eyes, set too close together and not too big. There were two ugly warts on the side of her chin, which she tried so hard to cover up with make-up. Her skin was very fair, and the light face powder she wore showed up the downy mustache on her upper lip.

4

Sarah stood back a little and looked at her figure. "I must be twenty pounds overweight," she thought. She felt the pads of fat over her hips and stomach. Her bones were small and with all that extra weight she looked like a plump pillow. She frowned at herself. "I've never really taken stock of myself before, of all of me, anyway." She saw herself quite clearly in the mirror. "I do look just like some little brown hen. I *don't* look like a—slick chick. I wonder . . . I wonder if I could do something about it."

The thought kept running through her mind all the time she was preparing dinner. Maybe she could take a course in fixing herself up from one of those self-improvement schools—she'd seen their ads now and then. Funny she hadn't ever thought of it before; but then George had never given her reason to, before.

"Not the type!" she muttered into the creamed vegetables. "Not the type!"

She was surprised at the sharpness of the sting.

Deep in thought and concentrating on her cooking at the same time, she didn't hear a sound in the kitchen. But suddenly two brown hands were clapped over her eyes.

A tell-tale giggle gave her captor away. "Helen, you minx, you won't get any dessert, if you don't let me go." Two strong arms hugged her tightly.

"What are we having for supper, Mother?" The girl laid her cool cheek against her mother's hot face. "Something real good?"

Sarah smiled into the bright brown eyes of her daughter. "We always have something good, don't we?"

"How soon do we eat? I'm starved." Helen walked over to the refrigerator. She found a piece of celery, and went into the dining room, chewing on the crisp stalk.

"Well, look at the sleeping beauty. Get up, Daddy. I'm home." Helen sat down on the arm of the chair and tweaked her Dad's nose.

George opened his eyes and grinned at his pride and joy. "Hi, glamour girl. Give me a bite?" Helen offered him what was left of the celery.

"Dinner ready?" He yawned, stood up and stretched.

"Almost." Then Helen asked, thoughtfully, "Daddy, has Mother ever wrapped you around her little finger?"

"Nope." Her father ran his hands over his bulging stomach. "And what's more no other female is going to either." He chucked her under the chin. "What have you got tucked away in that over-worked brain of yours?"

"Oh pooh, I wasn't thinking of you, Daddy! I was thinking about Ham." Ham was the current boy friend, and Helen was nearly always thinking about him.

"Poor Ham, what cruel fate is in store for him now?" George grinned down at her.

"He claims no woman is ever going to wrap him around her little finger, and naturally I have to meet the challenge." She followed her father into the dining room.

"Naturally, you couldn't let a mere man get the best of you." George took his place at the head of the table.

Sarah brought in the tea cart, and set the steaming dishes on the big table. "What's this I hear?" she asked laughingly.

"Daddy says you nor any other woman will ever wrap him around their little finger, and I've just got to show Ham that I can, except I just don't know the proper procedure." Helen turned a puzzled face to her mother. "How does one go about it?"

Sarah looked at George and shook her head, "That is a feat I have never accomplished. What do you say, dear?"

George cleared his throat, "Well, I would say," he announced, "that any man that lets a woman get him into a compromising situation, or wheedle something out of him against his will— well, that would be my definition of wrapping him around her finger."

"Sounds kind of involved, but I've got the idea, Daddy!" Helen filled her plate, and ate heartily but in unusual silence. George winked at his wife, and they both smiled, knowing that Helen was preoccupied with plans.

"All women are alike, always trying to get some poor devil in their clutches." George passed his plate for a second helping. "Except you, dear. You haven't given me too much trouble."

"Thank you, kind sir. I learned when I was first married that you were boss." Sarah dropped her eyes so that George would not see the tears that welled up in them.

"I don't think you have cause for any regrets, Honey. I've given you most everything you've ever wanted, haven't I?"

"Oh, no, you haven't, Daddy!" Helen exclaimed. "Last year Mother wanted that lovely mink coat, and you gave her a silver fox. There's quite a difference. And then she needs a new car, but I'll bet she won't get it." Helen shook her finger at her Dad.

"I'm not made out of money. What's wrong with the silver fox? Nothing. It looks nice on your mother." George looked over at Sarah for support.

She smiled at his belligerent tone. "It's very nice, George, but I really believe we could afford a new car. After all we have nearly twenty-five thousand in the bank." Sarah was surprised at her courage in putting the issue up to him so bluntly. Usually she just hinted.

"H-m-m-p!" He always snorted when anything annoyed him. "So we have some money saved, but I'm not drawing three or four thousand out just for a car. I want to play around with the stock market this winter. Maybe in the spring we'll look at a new buggy."

Helen laid her fork down and turned to her mother. "I guess that's what you would call a futile attempt to wrap someone around someone's finger."

Sarah said tiredly, "Yes dear, a futile attempt."

"Not to change the subject, but I hope you haven't planned anything for Friday night, Sarah?" George helped himself to more coffee.

"No dear, why?"

"Red Felder came home with me this evening. He's on the entertainment committee for the H.B.O.S. Club. I'm not a member, but they want me to make a speech, so I said I'd go."

"What's it supposed to be, a banquet, or a stag affair?" Sarah asked innocently.

"I understand it's going to be quite a shindig. He said I could bring you, but I told him you didn't care for such night-life." Sarah was sure then that George just didn't want her to go.

Helen looked quickly at her mother, and saw the unhappiness that flooded her face. "Daddy, I think you're just a stinker." She flounced out of the room, leaving her father staring after her with a baffled look on his face.

"Well, what brought that on?"

Sarah piled the dishes on the tea wagon, and left him to draw his own conclusions. It nearly floored him to have Helen criticize him.

Chapter 2

FRIDAY NIGHT SARAH HELPED GEORGE DRESS. SHE HELPED HIM WITH his bow tie, and as she smoothed the dinner jacket down, she was uncomfortably conscious of her hands—worn and rough and reddened. "My, you look nice, George. I'd love to hear you make that speech," she said.

George admired himself in the mirror, and patted his tummy. "Think I look too heavy in front?" he turned around to get a better view from the side.

Sarah cocked her head and looked at him from several different angles. "No-o, I don't think you look fat, George, but your waist line is a little snug." She ran her finger inside his trouser top.

George moved away from her impatiently. "Maybe we both ought to go on a diet."

Her face flamed red, but she held her tongue. "He's just touchy, because he's worried about his speech," she excused him to herself. But it hurt.

When he was ready to leave Helen came out of her room and fussed over him. "You look very distinguished, Daddy. Don't turn wolfish tonight. You've got a nasty gleam in your eyes."

George laughed self-consciously, pecked Helen on the cheek and kissed Sarah lightly on the lips. "Don't wait up for me, dear."

Sarah held the door open and said good-naturedly, "Have a

9

good time dear, but be careful." She and Helen stood in the door and watched him drive away in his company's car.

Helen put her arm through Sarah's. "How you can be so sweet and easy going, Mother, beats me! Believe me, no husband of mine, is going to go off and leave me alone whenever he feels like it."

"Let's hope your husband loves you enough, so he will want you to go with him, Baby."

Helen stared at her mother, unbelievingly, "You don't mean Daddy doesn't love you?"

"No, not exactly. He loves me in a selfish way. He likes my cooking; he knows I'm a good mother; I've been a true and faithful wife for twenty years; I keep his home clean; I take care of his clothes; I wait patiently for him to come home from his trips; I never show any jealousy of him or what he does or the fun he seems to have; I have scrimped and saved, to help him have this lovely home." Her eyes traveled over the rich furnishings. "But when he wants to go out, he never asks me. I'm just his little brown wren, his housekeeper." She was a little surprised at herself, talking this way to Helen, and she saw Helen's shock.

"It isn't fair, Mummy! Why don't you rear up on your hind legs and fight?"

"What's the use? He'd out-talk me." She sighed, "Besides, I took a good look at myself today, and I don't really blame him, Helen. I'm not much to show off."

"Why, Mother, you're the dearest, sweetest person in the whole world. You have the disposition of an angel. And besides, beauty isn't everything." She finished lamely; she sounded embarrassed.

"I don't have many attributes, do I?" Sarah rested her head on the back of the chair and closed her eyes. "I guess George has always been more conscious of my lack of charm and beauty than I have been. I really never thought much about it, until today."

Helen patted her hand in sympathy, and Sarah went on, "I've been so busy; raising you, taking care of the house and yard,

10

taking care of *him*. And I never had any reason to worry much about what I looked like. I was always under the impression that George loved me for myself, but I can see now that he just loves me for what I can do for him, and for what I stand for; security and a refuge when he wants to come back to the nest." Her tone was bitter and her face was lined with tiredness.

Helen picked up one of her mother's hands and examined it. "You ought to be ashamed to let your hands get into such a condition, Mother. You could wear gloves when you work in the yard." She couldn't bear to see her mother look so crushed, but being Helen, she had to be honest. "And you could diet, Mother, you're much too fat for your height."

"Yes, I suppose I've just let myself go."

"Why don't you join a reducing class? There ought to be something you could do, to open Daddy's eyes."

"I don't know, I'll think about it. I'll have to think." She picked up the evening paper and looked over the advertisements: School of Beauty; School for Models; Reducing Salon; Glamour School; Dancing School.

Ham came to see Helen, and Sarah excused herself. They were probably delighted. She smiled in silent amusement upon realizing they were both too nice to sulk if she stayed.

Sarah sat in the den for a long time. Her mind kept going around in circles, searching for something, or some way, to ease her mind; to help her solve the problem that confronted her. "Maybe it's no more of a problem now than it was ten years ago, only I have a hunch that it is—that in a little while our marriage will—well, run into a crossroads at least. He could so easily meet and get interested in a beautiful woman, or any other woman with more than I've got."

She recalled again his words to his friend, his dutiful pecking that was scarcely a kiss, his pleasure in going somewhere without her. She sighed. "I've got to beat him to the punch. Oh, but can I?"

Chapter 3

MONDAY MORNING SARAH GOT UP EARLY TO GET GEORGE OFF TO THE big sales meeting. Whenever he was home, the home office gave him the floor. For six years he had been the Big Boy over the rest of the salesmen in the State of Illinois. At forty-five George had accomplished as much as most men had when they were in their sixties. He expounded the theory of his success to Sarah, boasting, "Yes sir, not many men my age make ten thousand a year, my dear." He helped himself to another egg. "I'll have to go over my talk before I leave."

Sarah glanced at the kitchen clock. "Then you'd better hurry, George! It's a long way to Michigan Avenue."

"They'll wait for me." He left the table and went into the den.

Helen drifted into the breakfast room, still half asleep. "Gee, I wish I didn't have to go to school today Mother. Tests and more tests."

"You really should rest more over the week-end, dear." Sarah never scolded, just suggested. Helen had always been a docile child, usually taking her mother's kindly hints the way they were meant.

Now she answered, "You're so right, Mother, but then I'll make up for it this week. I told Ham no dates this week. I've got to cram." She ate a good breakfast, for which Sarah was thank-

12

ful. Slim as a string bean, Helen never worried about food as long as there was plenty to eat.

Sarah watched her daughter clean her plate, and laughed softly. "I envy you, you enjoy eating so much. I wish I could eat and stay slim."

"Are you going on a diet, Mother?" Helen raised interested eyes to her mother's worried face.

"I'm going to do something; I don't know just where to begin." She began to clear the table. "Would you mind very much if I have Dora prepare dinner tonight?" Dora was the colored woman who came in to clean and do the laundry. Once in a while Sarah had her cook a few meals, but Helen and George didn't like her cooking.

Now Helen made a little face. "Oh, if it will help you out, Mother, I guess I can stand that southern concoction she calls food."

"I'll plan the meal. She's not so bad, if I sort of steer her in the right direction." Sarah thought to herself, "You might as well get used to it, I'll be too busy to cook." Aloud she remarked, "I'm going down to the Loop this morning. I'll probably be gone all day."

A horn sounded out in front, Helen jumped to her feet, "There's Ham, I've got to scram." She planted a wet kiss on her mother's face. "Have fun, darling, and don't try to lose it all in one day." She rushed into the other room and grabbed her books, and like a breeze flew out the door.

George came out and exclaimed irritably. "What was that?"

"Your daughter leaving for school."

"She didn't say good-bye to her poor old Dad."

Sarah laughed. "I guess she forgot you were home, dear."

"H-m-m-p. Well, I'll have to get along, Sarah. What are you going to do?"

"Dora comes today. Don't worry, I'll keep busy." Sarah raised her face for his kiss. "Will you be home early?"

"I'll probably be tied up most of the day, going over reports, but I'll be home for dinner."

13

Sarah watched her husband walk to his car parked in the driveway. He tried to look so important. She wondered how he impressed other women. There had been flaming red lipstick smeared on the hankerchief he had carried to the banquet Friday night. It had worried her all week-end. Was that an everyday occurrence, kissing other women, or being kissed? Did he carry on with the other sex while he was away from home? Maybe it was too late to do anything. Sarah washed the dishes, while she waited for Dora. She wondered where she should begin to solve her problems. It looked hopeless at the moment.

It was after nine when she left her cozy Northside home. Chicago traffic was a little too fast for Sarah; she drove to the elevated and parked her car. She'd make better time taking the "L" she told herself. Besides it was cheaper. Then: "Why don't you quit kidding yourself, Sarah Davis? You're just plain scared. Afraid to drive, afraid to talk, afraid to stick up for yourself! Afraid of George and his criticisms." Her thoughts stabbed at her nastily, as she climbed the elevated steps.

Several men were on the platform waiting for the Loop express. One quick look at Sarah and they went back to their newspapers. No second looks. Just once in her life she'd like to command respect and attention. It must be fun to have strange men flirt with you, whistle at you. Never once in her forty years had such things happened to her. George had been the only man in her life. She had felt flattered that he had singled her out. Maybe she would have been an old maid, if she hadn't married George.

The express stopped fleetingly; she hurried aboard, found a seat next to a smart-looking blonde. Most of the male eyes, Sarah noticed, were turned her way. Well, the girl was striking. Beige suit, black accessories, nice skin and soft white hands. She had an air of glamour about her.

Sarah shrank down in her corner. How dowdy she must look in her plain black suit, flat heeled oxfords, rough red hands holding the large ostrich bag that George had brought back from California; a bag that would last the rest of her life. It was like

14

a caterpillar and a butterfly sitting together. It just wasn't fair; there must be some way to even things up.

Sarah breathed a sigh of relief when the train screeched to a stop. She got off and hurried down to the busy street. Then she stopped for she had no idea where to go or what to do first.

She stood at the corner looking about her. There was a beautician's sign on a side street. "I could go in and have a shampoo and a manicure, while I make some sort of decision," she thought. She hoped they could take her without an appointment.

The shop was deserted. An operator hurried towards her and then checked the schedule. "Guess I can work you in before my next customer. This way." Sarah followed the trim white figure.

It felt so good to have a professional shampoo. "Just towel-dry it please, then my bangs and sides will lay flat," Sarah suggested as the girl finished the last rinse.

"Don't you use any rinse on your hair, Madam?"

Sarah shook her head.

"Well, you should! You have lots of gray showing."

Sarah sighed. "I need more than a rinse, my dear. Maybe you would have some idea what I should do."

That was an opening. While the pert young miss skillfully manicured her neglected nails, Sarah sadly confided her woes. The girl stopped now and then and looked at her. She seemed really interested and yet she must hear a lot of such talk. When Sarah had finished, the girl said, "What you need, honey, is the works. A complete overhaul."

She pursed her lips, thinking, wracking her brain, for some information she had tucked away. "Wait, I know of a very exclusive place on Madison Street that does some sort of glamourizing. I'll call them."

In a few minutes she was back. "I made an appointment for you at eleven o'clock. I think they can help you." She wrote the name and address on one of her cards. "Do you have plenty of money?"

Sarah nodded.

"Good, I think their fees run high. Come back and let me

15

know what goes on." She patted Sarah as she accompanied her to the door.

"Oh, I will, dear, you've been an angel. Maybe this is what I'm looking for."

Sarah had a few minutes before the appointment. She went into a small café and ordered coffee so that she could think. She had to think about money. "I've still got what Papa gave me when he died. He said I should keep it for an emergency. Well, I guess you'd call this an emergency. I wouldn't dare ask George for any. I'll just go whole hog, if I have to."

The foyer of the Madison Street building had recessed alcoves, filled with pictures of beautiful models; dancing, posing and reclining. Most of the pictures were of girls, but here and there a handsome male model was on display. Paul Domere's Glamour Salon; probably a modeling school. Well, she might as well go up and talk to them. If they couldn't help, maybe they knew someone that could.

Apparently the Salon occupied the entire fourteenth floor. Sarah walked down the hall until she came to a large modernistic lounge. Then she approached the woman at the desk, hesitating a little because the other woman looked so forbidding.

"Yes, Madam, what can I do for you?" Sarah felt the receptionist eyeing her. 'What in the world is that creature doing here?' the expression seemed to say.

"I'm Mrs. George Davis, I made an appointment for eleven o'clock. I'm not sure if this sort of thing is what I'm looking for." She smiled a wistful smile at the stern face back of the imposing desk.

"Just what sort of thing are you looking for?" The woman waved a red-tipped hand in Sarah's direction. "Suppose you sit down and tell me all about it." She didn't look or sound so formidable when she unbent a little.

So for the second time that morning Sarah unloaded her worries to a perfect stranger. She finished with "So, I'm looking for someone to help me make myself over, completely, from my head to my toes."

16

Sarah was surprised to hear the other woman laugh so heartily. "Sounds like fun, honey. Let me call Mr. Domere in here." She pushed a buzzer and very shortly the dapper Paul Domere stood in front of Sarah. He nodded at her when the receptionist introduced them, then she quickly told him Sarah's story.

He frowned and shook his head. "I don't see how we can help. You see, Madam, this is a school for actresses, actors, models, dancers and even movie stars. We teach them modeling, all the social graces, dancing, everything and anything to prepare them for their careers. Diets, horseback riding, public speaking, even plastic surgery."

Sarah's eyes lit up. "Oh, it sounds like what I need! I'm not an artist, and I'm not looking for any career, but I do want to be beautiful." She looked so forlorn, begging him for the chance to be reborn. "Won't you take me? I have plenty of money to pay for your help."

The woman at the desk added her plea, "Oh, come on, Mr. Domere, you have turned out so many beautiful models—see what you can do for Mrs. Davis. I think she deserves a chance at happiness."

Domere studied Sarah's sincere face. She actually looked pathetic. "All right; I'll try to do my best. But you must coöperate fully, if you want to be a success, Mrs. Davis." He was warning her, firmly. The school was strict, the courses rigorous.

Sarah clasped her hands in front of her. "Oh I will! Anything you say."

Then he, too, seemed to unbend. He smiled. "We'll go into my private office and confer with Dr. Bloom."

Sarah followed him into an inner room. He left her alone for two minutes, and suddenly a uniformed nurse stuck her head in the door and asked, "Mrs. Davis, come with me please."

She took Sarah into a hospital room, gleaming white. "Please disrobe and put this gown on."

Sarah's eyes widened in surprise. "Why should I undress?"

"Because Dr. Bloom must see just where, and how much plastic surgery you'll need. You needn't be afraid. You'd be sur-

17

prised how many women have their faces lifted, their busts, stomachs and so on." She chatted away as she helped Sarah get out of her clothes.

"I guess I just hadn't thought that far ahead," Sarah murmured. What was she getting into? Lifted faces, busts and so on?

Dr. Bloom had Sarah lie flat on a table, while he made his examination. "M-m-m, take these notes, Miss Stone. Facial plastic, lift cheeks, straighten nose, lift chin, remove warts and hair. We'll give you a new hairline, also thin and arch your eyebrows, Mrs. Davis. They're completely out of line for your facial structure. Remove hair from upper lip, arm pits, forearms and legs." The doctor pulled her gown down. "Bust, stomach—M-m-m—I guess that's all." He pushed Sarah's hair back. "Oh, ears, too, Miss Stone. It won't hurt a bit, and in a week it will be completely healed. When do you want to start, Mrs. Davis?"

He waited as Sarah sat up. Her head was whirling, things were moving too fast.

"I don't know, doctor, I hadn't dreamed of anything like this. I'm afraid this part would have to come last."

"Well, you make your plans with Mr. Domere and whenever you're ready for surgery, we'll be waiting."

Sarah murmured her thanks as he left the room. The nurse helped her into her clothes and then, ushering her back into Mr. Domere's office, handed him a copy of the notes she had taken.

Paul Domere waved Sarah into a chair beside his desk. "Now suppose we have a very frank talk, Mrs. Davis. You're sure you want to have a new face and a different personality, just because you want to hold your husband's love and interest?"

Sarah was surprised at his question. "Of course; I said I did."

"You'd be surprised, Mrs. Davis, how many requests we have from people who have prison records, are wanted by the police, or for some diabolic reason want to change into another character." He smiled at her horrified expression.

"I can give references," she declared, "or if you want to check up on me in any way, you're certainly welcome to. But it must be without my husband knowing. I want to keep this a secret until I'm a finished product."

"Give me a short resumé of your daily habits, life, likes, desires and so on." He tipped his swivel chair back and waited for Sarah to begin.

She laughed softly, "I feel as though I'm on trial for my life."

"You are, you're pleading for a new one." He smiled at her again. "Relax, Mrs. Davis. I'm on your side. What have you to tell me?"

"Well, I'm just a plain housewife. I cook, clean and take care of my daughter Helen (she's sixteen). My husband travels a lot. Supervisor for the International Match Company. He really is a key man, but he makes me mad sometimes, the way he brags. When he's home he doesn't want to go out, or take me out. If he goes out, he makes it plain he doesn't want me along. I don't smoke, drink, play cards, or dance. I have a rose garden for a hobby. I used to play the piano a little, church hymns and classics. I belong to a Woman's Club and attend the P.T.A., but I don't take an active part. I'm too shy. I've always been afraid to get up and express myself."

She sighed. "I have no close friends, not even a really good woman friend. I wear dark, conservative clothes. I'm a very good manager, but I really have no desire for a business career. I don't care much for make-up or anything artificial. I went to a finishing school in Alabama. I don't like people that pretend to do one thing and then turn around and do something different. This great desire I have for beauty and recognition has become an obsession. Is there anything else you want to know?" She laughed self-consciously. "I didn't know I could talk so much."

"That just about covers everything, Mrs. Davis. First, we're going to change your whole outlook on life. We'll start gradually. Just how much time do we have before you spring the surprise on your husband?"

"I'd like to be all ready the first part of December."

"That gives us three months. As I said before, most of it

depends on you. You're going to pay dearly for it, so get all you can out of it."

He made a few notes on a pad. "We'll start with diet, exercise, steam baths, massages, horseback riding, dancing and whatever we can work in in an eight hour stretch. Can you come each day, say nine to six?"

"Whatever you say, Mr. Domere. What can I expect for my money and time and coöperation?" She had to be reassured.

He laughed at her anxious face. "We've turned out some pretty fair models; I'm sure we'll surprise even ourselves in your case, Mrs. Davis. In my department, I'll see that you have a lovely figure, a complete course in all the social arts, and know how to stand and walk—things a model must know. Dr. Bloom is one of the finest surgeons in his field. He'll draw you several pictures before he operates to show you the structural outline of your face after surgery. You can choose your own face. The fee will be fifteen hundred dollars in advance. You will start in the morning. Any questions?"

Fifteen hundred! But—no, she'd vowed to do it. She answered, "So many that my head is buzzing, but I'll ask them as we go along. I don't mind paying your price, Mr. Domere, if I can be sure that this overhauling job will get results."

"We'll knock your husband's eyes out."

Sarah Davis giggled at the threat.

Chapter 4

SARAH ARRIVED HOME IN A DITHER. SHE HAD STOPPED AT THE BANK and taken the five thousand dollars her father had left her, and deposited it in her own checking account. She had one for the monthly bills and the allowance that George gave her each month. George had one of his own—where he kept most of their money. She knew how much they had saved, but she didn't have access to it. As long as he made the money, George felt, he was entitled to the handling of it. So he doled out a certain amount to Sarah each month, to run the house and take care of incidentals, and if she needed clothes, he gave her more. He wasn't stingy, he was just careful. Sarah felt a little sick when she thought of handing all that money to Mr. Domere in the morning. George would die ten deaths if he ever found out about it. She felt a little hysterical. If George only knew what she had gotten herself into!

She was very quiet during dinner. It was nice to come home and find a clean house and a hot meal waiting for her, but George grumbled about the greasy fried chicken. "As a cook, Dora makes a good laundress."

"S-h-h, it's not too bad. I rather enjoy having someone wait on me once in a while," Sarah declared.

George looked over the rim of his glasses, and studied Sarah's

21

bland expression. That remark she made had all the earmarks of a dig.

After dinner, when Helen had gone into her room to study, George settled himself in his favorite chair and lit a cigar. He waited until Sarah came back from the kitchen and then he asked, "Can you spare a minute, dear? Something came up at the office today that requires me to start rolling again."

Sarah had worried all day, wondering how she would manage being away from home so much. Now George's words lifted a weight from her shoulders.

"But you just came home, George." She mustn't be too anxious.

"I know it honey, but after all I'm supervisor. What I want to tell you is, that I'll be gone much longer this time. I have three month's work in front of me. I'll fly home at least once a month, though."

He looked at Sarah, but she said nothing. "I'll be home to spend the Christmas holidays, anyway." He sounded apologetic.

"That'll be nice, George." Sarah picked up the evening paper and glanced through it.

Things didn't ring quite true to George. Sarah had always gone into their room and cried a little. Tonight she acted as though she didn't care. "You don't seem to be bothered by my going away." He acted just a little bit disappointed.

"Well, George, you always said it was your job, and in time I'd get used to it. So-o, I guess I'm just getting used to it."

"H-m-m-p! I'll call you now and then."

"If you call, be sure it's in the evening, I'll be busy working in the yard and going to my typing class. I might miss you." She smiled to herself back of the paper. What a surprise he was in for. It was like standing on the threshold of a new life. Why, both of them were.

Helen came out and sat on the foot stool near her father's chair. "Daddy, have you read 'Dark Kisses'?"

He looked over his glasses, and shook his head.

"You should, it's dreamy." She sat staring for a few seconds at

22

her Dad's smoking cigar. "What would you do, Mother, if Daddy had an affair with another woman and you found out about it?"

George Davis choked, sputtered, removed his cigar and carefully laid it in the ash tray. "Here, let me see that book, young lady! What kind of trash are you reading?"

He thumbed through the novel, " 'Darling, come with me tonight to my little cabin in the woods. No one will know where we are and I'll have you all to myself. He bent his handsome head and kissed her tenderly.' "

George snorted disdainfully, "Bosh! What corn! Where did you get this thing?"

Helen reached for it. "I got it out of the school library. I have to make a book report on it."

George roared with laughter, then snorted again. Helen grinned at him, then repeated her question to Sarah. "What would you do, if Daddy was indiscreet?"

George's fat face became redder than red. Sarah, eyeing him thoughtfully said, "Well, I've never thought much about a situation like that; I've always trusted your father implicitly. But," she spoke slowly, and very distinctly, so it would sink in, "if I had definite proof that your father had betrayed my trust and love, I'd get a divorce."

"Oh for corn's sake, Sarah, I've never cheated on you, and I'm not going to begin now." He picked up his cigar and puffed hard on it. "I hope you don't waste your time reading such stuff and nonsense as Helen is doing." He glared in Sarah's direction. "It seems to me you should supervise her selection of books a little more closely."

"I'm sure if the school approves of the book, it can't be too bad." Sarah went back to her paper, then added matter-of-factly, "Besides, it won't hurt her to get a little knowledge of the relationships between a man and woman."

A cloud of smoke billowed to the ceiling.

"Why, Mother, I didn't know you were so broadminded. I'll tell you something. Next year when I'm a senior, I'm going to

23

take a course in Sex, Marriage, Child Care and whatever else pertains to the career of a wife."

"I think it's a grand idea, dear. When I think of all the things I didn't know, and found out the hard way, I shudder. I'm glad you'll be better prepared to meet the issues every woman has to face with a man."

George was staring at her. "What's gotten into you, Sarah? If you had no other virtues, I've always been proud that my wife was a perfect lady. A perfect lady in every respect." He thumped gently on the arm of his chair to emphasize his statement.

The perfect lady smiled and murmured her thanks. "I was just an old-fashioned girl brought up in an old maid's school, learning just enough to keep me from being a complete idiot. Well, I'm glad Helen has all of the advantages and fun I never had."

Ham came in at that moment and the discussion was dropped. Sarah was relieved, and George looked as if he were, too.

Sarah went out to the kitchen to get things organized for breakfast. From now on it would be nip and tuck, to get Helen off to school, and to get down to the Loop at nine o'clock every day. But it would be fun, and each day would be a gay adventure, even if she had to pay through the nose for it.

She was setting the table, when George joined her. "Whee, I like music, but football chants are too much for me." He sat down at the table. The house rocked with the noise from Ham's bass voice, stomping feet and Helen's flying fingers on the piano. "We should build a rumpus room in the basement if we are in for jam sessions every night," George grumbled.

"I think that would be a good idea, George. After all, Helen has to have some place to have fun. We could get an old upright and let them go to town. Coffee?"

His eyes followed Sarah as she moved around the kitchen. "You know, dear, you're getting awfully broad in the back." He slapped her as she went past him. It hurt her feelings to have him make fun, but it would soon be different.

24

Chapter 5

SARAH WAS UP WITH THE BIRDS THE NEXT MORNING. SHE TOOK HER bath, dressed and put on a clean wrapper. It did absolutely nothing for her. She grimaced at herself as she fixed her hair, and put the usual dab of powder on her face. "There, now, I'm all ready to go, except for my suit. I hope George is in a hurry to leave."

She rushed around preparing breakfast.

George came out to the kitchen, yawning and groaning. "I know fall is here when my rheumatism starts hitting me. I'll have to eat and run, dear. I sure hate to drive all day, but that's the life of a salesman." He sat down and tucked his napkin in his belt. "Waffles and sausages, Sarah?"

"Yes dear, I thought you'd need a good breakfast to travel on."

"I'll really miss your cooking while I'm gone." He sighed; food was a big factor in his life.

Sarah asked softly, "Is that all you'll miss, George?" She poured herself a cup of coffee, and sat down across the table from him. Her light blue eyes were bright, her cheeks were flushed; she was so keyed up she felt as if she'd burst. How could she keep her secret for three months? She was so excited she couldn't eat a bite.

She was conscious of George's scrutinizing gaze. She'd have to be careful.

25

He said, "Do you feel well dear? Your face is flushed and your eyes look like you have a fever." He reached across the table and picked up her little rough hand. "I'll miss you and Helen so much; sometimes I wish I had been a plumber or a factory worker. Then I'd never have to leave home." He squeezed her hand. "Helen even forgets me when I'm home." He sounded sad, and middle-aged.

Sarah laughed and jumped up, exclaiming. "Oh, come now, George, let's don't get melancholy. Have another cup of coffee while I get our child started for school." She left, talking to herself, "Honestly I believe she'd drown if I didn't go in and pull her out."

Dora came in the back door, as George went out the front. Helen joined her mother at the front door, to wave farewell to George. Sarah really did hate to see him go, and he did sound sincere about missing them. Maybe he was having a change of heart in his old age. Or maybe it was the weather, cold, wet and dreary—made a person long for his warm, cheerful home.

Sarah jerked herself back to the realities of the day. "Got to get going, darling. I'll be at Paul Domere's Salon if you need me."

She rushed into her bedroom and slipped into her plain black suit, grabbed her hat and put it on as she made her way to the front door. "Dora, there's a list of groceries to order, and just do the general cleaning today. Be careful going to school, Helen. Be seeing you." She pecked her daughter's cheek, and was off on her big adventure.

The elevated was crowded with early morning shoppers and white collar workers. Sarah hung on a strap all the way to the Loop, but she didn't mind for her thoughts were flying as fast as the wheels of the train. What would she have to do first? Would she be in a class with others? They'd probably make fun of her. Her eyes travelled over the other passengers. Fresh young faces, smart matrons, slick chicks. Sarah smiled smugly. One of these days, she'd be able to stand up beside them.

The clock struck nine as she walked into the Salon lounge.

26

The receptionist greeted her with a friendly grin. "Good morning, Cinderella. I thought maybe you'd change your mind overnight."

"Good morning. No, I'm determined to change my spots."

"I'm Mrs. Thackery; everybody gets familiar around here and calls me Thack."

"I'm Sarah."

Thack took Sarah by the arm. "Come on, I'll show you the dressing rooms." They entered a clean, modern room with dressing tables, lockers and a couple of chaise lounges and chairs.

"Here's an empty locker and here's a playsuit. M-m-m, size eighteen, that ought to do it." She took Sarah's raincoat and hung it up. "Got any money in your bag?"

"A little." Sarah was pulling the sunsuit over her fat hips. "Why?"

"Better park it with me, we have too many light-fingered friends around here. Any time you have something valuable along, just give it to me."

"Thank you, that's very kind of you." Sarah looked at the older woman gratefully. "Can you give me some sort of resumé of what I'm in for this morning?" Her laugh was strained.

"You mean the low-down on your transformation?" Thack settled herself comfortably on a chaise lounge. "Well, you'll be put on a diet, get a stiff work-out for an hour. Then the steam cabinet. Old Lil will give you a going over. Massage." She lit a cigarette. "Have one?" She held the case out to Sarah.

"No thank—wait, let me try one. I've never smoked before, but I must learn." She giggled as Thack held the lighter for her.

"Just put it in your mouth and start puffing."

Sarah tried puffing cautiously. "Ugh, it doesn't taste very good. Maybe it's because I haven't had anything to eat." She laid the cigarette in a tray.

"You'd be better off if you never started the habit."

A bell sounded and Thack stood up. "That's the boss. Come on, he'll start you off."

27

Mr. Domere met Sarah with outstretched hand. "All ready and willing?"

"Very. I've brought you a check. May I have a receipt, stating the full terms of our agreement?" Sarah sat on the edge of her chair, looking prim and yet ridiculous in the starched playsuit.

Domere laughed. "You're still a little skeptical about this business being on the up and up. Well, I don't blame you. Fifteen hundred dollars is a lot of money to hand over on a mere promise, but that's all I can do—make promises to you. You know though—we'll do our very best to turn you into a butterfly."

Sarah took the check from her bag and handed it to him. "I'll take my chances."

"Have you had your breakfast?" He rang a buzzer on his desk, then looked at Sarah.

"No, I was too excited to eat."

"Good. I want Dr. Bloom to check you over and give you a diet. You'll eat breakfast at home. Lunch here, and dinner at home. No eating between meals. In other words, if you cheat, Mrs. Davis, the cause is lost. You have to meet us half way."

"Mr. Domere, I know that, and this project means too much to me for me to spoil it."

He laughed and gave her a searching look. "We'll see. It's easy to say, but you'll have your temptations. Ah, here's the doctor. Better check Mrs. Davis, doctor, before she starts our diet and reducing treatment. I wouldn't want it to be too much for her."

Doctor Bloom listened to her heart, breathing, took her blood pressure, asked her some questions about her past medical history, and then turned to Domere. "Sound as a dollar. I guess she can take it." Sarah was handed a menu for the week. "You are allowed twelve hundred calories a day, for the first week. Follow it as closely as possible. You may substitute different greens, salads, vegetables and meat, but don't add anything. Understand?"

Domere acknowledged Sarah's nod with, "All right, let's go to the gym. There are several others taking calisthenics. Dancers,

28

models, prize fighters, and one housewife." He grinned down at her.

"If you get tired just quit." He ushered her into the big room equipped with swings, bars, horses, ladders, punching bags, pulleys, rowing machines; so many gadgets that Sarah felt like turning around and running away.

A big man in trunks came towards her and asked, "Mrs. Davis?"

Sarah could only nod her head; she was frightened. Would she have to climb those ladders and hang by her feet like those two men are doing?

The big man was saying, "Just call me Sam. Now don't be afraid. I won't expect you to be a monkey yet." His eyes followed her terrified gaze to a rope walker balancing himself above their heads. "You'll be rubbing shoulders with all kinds of freaks." Sarah followed him across the floor; he found a mat for her and then said, "Better take your shoes off, and wear sneakers tomorrow. Say," he patted her on the hip, "got a girdle on?"

Sarah shied away from him. "Of course." Her face reddened from his familiarity. Even George rarely took such liberties.

"Well, you better get rid of it. You can't build a body up with an iron fence around it." He pointed to the mat, "Stand on that, and just try to do what I tell you."

The rest of the class found their respective places and waited for Sam to sound off.

"Okay, hands on hips. On the count of one, bend left; count two, bend right; three, touch toes. Like this. Let's go; one—two —three—one—two—three. Hold it." He walked towards Sarah. "Don't you know which is right and which is left?"

"I'm sorry, I just got mixed up." She felt like crawling under the pad.

"Okay, let's go. One—two—three—one—two—three. Left, right, toes, bend, bend, down. Bend, I said! One—two—" Sam kept counting until Sarah was out of breath.

"Okay, let's try this." He did a stooping exercise. "Let's go." Sarah nearly split the seams in her girdle. She tried hard, but

29

she couldn't begin to stoop the way he wanted them to, so she sat down on her pad. Sam waved his hand, "Don't let it get you down, Mrs. Davis, you'll catch on. Okay, let's jump rope."

And so it went for nearly an hour. Sarah was up, then down, puffing, but trying. And she thought she'd drop, she was so tired.

Domere came and got her at the end of an hour. "Sam puts you through the mill, doesn't he?"

Sarah smiled wanly.

"The steam cabinet is next, then Lil. You'll get used to it, and then you'll enjoy it. The first week is always the hardest." To Lil he said, "Here she is, undress her."

Lil tucked her in a steam box, and Sarah's heart pounded so hard that the blood rushed to her head and she felt like a whirling dervish. The walls, the cabinet and Lil went round and round. She gritted her teeth and closed her eyes; she wouldn't yell Uncle. When Lil opened the door and helped her out, she looked like an overheated lobster.

"M-m-m, first time I see such a red body and such a white face!" Lil draped a sheet around Sarah's shrinking form. "Are you feeling all right, lady?"

"I feel a little faint, but I think I'm just hungry." She struggled up to the table Lil indicated.

"First, I'll give you the massage, then maybe I can get you something to eat. This diet business is no fun."

Sarah grunted as Lil kneaded her shoulders. "This is my first morning. I haven't started a diet yet." It was easier to keep her mouth closed by not talking. Lil pounded, twisted, massaged, chopped first the back and then the front. The big Swedish woman laughed gleefully, or so Sarah thought. She seemed to take special delight in making Sarah groan.

She informed her, "The human body is almost fifty percent muscles. I don't think you ever used any of them."

Sarah opened her mouth to contradict her; she wanted to tell her how many it took to mow the lawn, to pull the weeds, to do the housework, but she thought, "Oh, what's the use?"

The big Swede slapped her buttocks with the flat of her hand,

30

a hard spanking. "You're soft, like a pillow. Take a lot of hard work to knock all that fat off."

Sarah let her body go limp; two big tears slipped off her cheeks and splashed on the floor. This was only the first day. Was it worth it? She had no idea she'd have to take such physical abuse. This woman was actually beating her up. She'd have to talk to Mr. Domere about it. "Okay lady, get your clothes and take a shower."

Lil deftly wrapped the sheet about her. Sarah stooped to pick up her clothes and she thought all fifty per cent of her muscles were torn loose. She moaned.

Lil pushed her into a shower stall, turned the steaming water on, and grinned at the timid woman standing in front of her. "You'll get used to it, first thing you know, you'll come in and say, 'Lil, give me the works.'"

Sarah shook her head at the closed door. "Not me." The shower felt good and soothed her aching body. She just wanted to stand there and let the water pour over her and heal her bruised body and her bruised feelings.

Someone pounded on the door. "Come out, lady, I've got some coffee."

It took Sarah five minutes to get into her girdle. She must be swollen. "I'll be so glad when I can throw you in the garbage can!" She said it viciously through clenched teeth. She pushed, pulled and struggled until she had all the rolls of fat tucked away. "It's going to take a lot of pounding to knock all that fat off," Lil had said. Sarah flinched. How could she stand it, day after day? "Fifteen hundred dollars says I've got to," she murmured.

"Hurry up, lady, cold coffee is no good." Lil's voice boomed through the room.

"Sorry, Lil, I just couldn't get my girdle on." Sarah apologized as she tried to pat her hair back in place.

"Body is wet. What for do you want to be made over?" She looked closely at Sarah who was modestly trying to pull her play suit down to her knees.

31

"Here drink your coffee. Toast?" Lil held a plate with two pieces of dry toast on it. The coffee was black.

"Dry toast?" She bit a piece off gingerly. "No butter or jelly?" She looked hopefully at Lil.

"Too fattening. No cream, no butter, no sweets, no cheating. Why do you do it, huh?"

Sarah thought, "I'm ugly? George should see Lil!" She answered Lil's question, thoughtfully. "Vanity, Lil, just plain vanity. I've got a lovely home, a beautiful daughter, money and a nice husband, but I want to be beautiful for my man."

"Why? Does he like pretty faces? Coke bottle shapes?" She took her big bony hands and made an eye picture for Sarah.

Sarah took a big gulp of the hot black coffee before she answered, "I'm not sure, Lil, but I think so. I wouldn't stand a chance if it came right down to any competition. That's why I want to be prepared."

Lil shrugged. "Bring him down here, I fix him." She grinned wickedly at Sarah. "I pound him up good."

"I'll bet you would." Sarah had a mental picture of George getting the works. She giggled. "I'd like to see that, Lil, but it wouldn't solve my problem, I'm afraid. I've just got to be made beautiful." She reached for the other piece of toast, cold and soggy by now, but filling. "How much weight do I have to lose, Lil?"

"Mr. Domere say thirty pounds. That takes a long time, lots of hard work. I give you sun bath tomorrow, make you nice and brown. Keep you from catching cold."

"This has more angles than I thought." Sarah looked at the scales. "If I cheat can you tell?"

"No, the scales can. You must lose two or three pounds a week, or exercise more." Lil laughed. "That Sam's a mean boy. He'll make you ride horseback, jump rope, bicycle all day." Lil picked up the dishes. "Better to starve."

"I agree with you." Sarah ran her hand down her aching hips.

"Now for a good treatment. Come." Lil beckoned.

Down the hall to a room marked Beauty Shop. Lil opened the

door and yelled, "May—the lady for a facial." She patted Sarah's shoulder in a friendly way. "Go on in. May'll take care of you."

It was wonderful to be able to relax and have gentle hands massage sweet smelling creams and lotions on her face, neck, arms and hands. It had been so long since she had a thoroughly good facial. May had just the right touch. She was a pleasant quiet girl. The first one Sarah felt she could be herself with. No tension or fear here. She sighed and relaxed completely. "That's good, Mrs. Davis. That's the secret of all good facials, complete relaxation. That's why I don't talk too much."

Sarah smiled at the friendly face bent over her. "Just let me ask one question. Why do I get facials if they are going to do plastic surgery?"

"Your skin has been neglected. It's got to be massaged and softened, so it won't look old and dry. Too many women have their hair and nails done faithfully every week but never think about their poor abused face. They just cover it up with make-up day in and day out, and finally they wake up with creepy necks, and dry, rough, sallow complexions. And then it's usually too late." She reached for more cream and worked on Sarah's forehead.

"I guess mine is in bad condition?"

"Well, not too bad. You have fine pores, not too many blackheads. The plastic surgery will remove all the wrinkles and lift your sagging jowls." She lifted Sarah's cheeks with a quick stroke. "All you really need is to get your skin softened and stimulated. I'll give you some electric facials that will help. Now close your eyes and rest."

Sarah closed her eyes and almost went to sleep. May wrapped hot oil pads around each blunt finger. Then she used a wringing motion up and down Sarah's arms. The treatment lasted until noon.

After she had dressed for the third time that morning, Sarah was ushered back to the ladies' rest room. Lil came bearing a tray with her lunch. "Here's your rabbit food, lady." She set the tray down beside Sarah's chair. "Eat hearty." Her laugh filled the room.

Sarah looked at her lunch; two lettuce leaves, a small baked potato, half a cup of carrots, a sliver of roast beef, a glass of skimmed milk and a half broiled grapefruit. She made a face, but she was so starved she wasted no time in longing for something better.

The two dancers that had been in the gym came in. One said, "Well look what's here." She stared at Sarah and then made a dash for the rest room. "When you got to go, you gotta go."

The other girl said, "Don't pay any attention to her, she's harmless. I'm Jill." She sat down next to Sarah and lit a cigarette.

"I'm Sarah. Are you on a diet?"

"Yeah, to get fat. But I can't. I eat every two hours, but I can't gain a pound." She blew a puff of smoke out of her perfect lips. "I dance it all off."

"I've got to lose thirty pounds in three months."

"What happens in three months?" Jill removed her shoes and massaged her toes.

Sarah's stomach got sort of squeamish. Couldn't the girl see she was trying to eat. The girl Jill kept right on playing with her feet. Sarah pushed her tray back and sipped on her milk. The girl looked up waiting for Sarah to answer her question.

"Oh yes, well I just have plans for a new life in three months."

"Yeah, Lil says you are going to be made over. If I had the money I'd have Doc Bloom fix my mouth."

"Why I think your mouth is lovely." Sarah looked at Jill's lips closely. "What's wrong with it."

"I've got a harelip, small, but it's there. I cover it up with lipstick and no one's the wiser."

"Oh that's too bad." Sarah finished her milk and looked at the clock. "I wonder what I'll have to do this afternoon."

"We all have certain routines to follow, but you'll probably have private instruction. Lil says you're loaded." She looked at Sarah enviously.

"I'm loaded?"

"Yeah, lots of money."

"Oh, I see. Well, perhaps I have enough, but I'm not rich."

The other girl came out of the rest room. "How about getting our lunch Jill?"

"Okay, but first meet Sarah. This is Irene. We both dance in the chorus at the Oriental." Jill walked towards the door. "We come up here between acts."

Sarah nodded at Irene. "It must be fun to be young and a chorus girl. I think that is every young girl's first dream." Sarah looked at both of them kindly.

Irene turned on her heel and said irritably. "Can it sister. It's no dream, just a lot of hoofing." She swept out the door.

"Like I said before, don't pay any attention to Irene. She's a nice kid, when you know her." She waved to Sarah as she left.

"M-m-m, what pleasant companions I'm going to have." She closed her eyes and rested. Her mind was busy wondering; what was Helen doing all day—where was George having his lunch—what was going to happen to her next. She wasn't kept in doubt long. Mr. Domere opened the door and announced:

"Mrs. Davis, your presence is now wanted in the ball room."

"The ball room, what for?" Sarah was astounded. A ball room.

"First I want to outline your social life and then you are going dancing."

"In the middle of the afternoon?"

"You've got to start some time Mrs. Davis. Here we are." He opened the door to a small room with a slick floor. There was a desk and a few chairs on one side of the room. A phonograph in the corner. Domere sat down at the desk and took out a pad and pencil. "Now what sort of dance steps do you want to learn?"

Sarah concentrated, "George likes to waltz, foxtrot, two step and I don't know Mr. Domere, I've never danced. I wouldn't know what to learn."

Mr. Domere shook his head in sympathy, "You've really wasted a lot of time, but we'll fix that." He patted her hand. "I'll have Mr. Grayson teach you all the old ones, but I think you should know how to rumba, samba, jitter-bug and do all the

35

new steps. Suppose you turn out to be that gorgeous woman you've been dreaming about, you'll have to be right up to date." He jotted down several things. Then he asked, "Does your husband play cards?"

"Oh, yes, he likes poker, canasta and gin rummy. Maybe I should learn to play cards too." She looked at Domere hopefully.

"That and a lot of other things." He pushed a button. Grayson came in and he waved Mrs. Davis into his arms. "Do a good job, Bob, I might want to take Mrs. Davis dancing some of these nights." He grinned at both of them.

Sarah's feet were made out of lead. All she could think, was, "If I was only younger. If I was only beautiful as I want to be, as I hope to be. Oh what a man." Bob Grayson was something to swoon over, and Sarah was still a woman. He was tall, dark and handsome. What's more he was about Sarah's age. He had a silver streak through his black hair. His warm brown eyes regarded her with as much respect and interest, as any other woman. Sarah was so flustered and flattered, she moved around in a trance.

Dimly his voice penetrated her mind, "Just relax and follow me. One, two, three—glide. One, two, three—glide." For one whole hour he held her in his arms. It was the biggest thrill she had had, for ages. If George could see her now. Mr. Grayson was saying in her ear, "You're as light as a feather, Mrs. Davis and you waltz beautifully. Tomorrow we'll try the fox-trot."

She came down out of the clouds when Mr. Domere came in with a lady. "How was the dancing?"

Sarah's mild blue eyes had a dazed look, her cheeks were flushed and she barely breathed the words, "It was wonderful."

Mr. Domere laughed, "Well let's hope you'll like your next lesson. This is Miss Baer. She's going to make a model out of you."

Miss Baer was a lovely person, close to forty, but so smart, chic and perfect, that she could pass for twenty. Sarah made up her mind that if she could be anything like Miss Baer, she wouldn't have to worry about other women. She walked, she sat down,

36

she stood up, they talked, they pretended, they played games, they had a lot of fun. Miss Baer told Sarah at the end of the lesson. "This is about the softest job I've ever had. You're a born lady, and that is about the hardest job I have; trying to turn would-be models into ladies. They are usually born, not made. Tomorrow I'll show you a few tricks of the trade. I might give you a job, who knows."

"You better wait until I get my new shape and face," Sarah warned.

"Just what do you want to be, a blonde, brunette or redhead?"

"Gee, I've just never thought about that. There's so many things for me to decide. What would you suggest?" Sarah's eyes went to Miss Baer's gray hair.

"Oh don't take me for an example. I've been gray for ten years or more."

"But I like it, I think you are one of the most attractive women I've seen for a long time."

"Thank you, coming from another woman, that's quite a compliment. But, to get back to you." She studied Sarah's face for a few minutes and then said, "We could use more seasoned models, that is matrons, in our business. You know we have a placing agency here, and some of the most exclusive shops are calling for older, more experienced women, especially if they have a lot of men buyers."

Sarah's hand fluttered to her throat, "You don't mean you'd actually give me a job modeling?" She was scared just thinking about it.

"Why not? 'Course that will be after we make you into that other person. I think you'd be stunning as a platinum blonde. Sort of on the silvery side. I'll have to talk to Domere and Dr. Bloom and see what we can figure out. You know, this is going to be fun."

After her modeling lesson, Mr. Domere took her to his office and showed Sarah how to play rummy, and talked to her about the things she was going to have to change, her habits, writing, name, mannerisms, laugh, way of speaking, idioms of speech and

37

so on. "We'll just have to practice every day for three months. You know, Mrs. Davis, when you first put this idea up to me, I took it purely as a business arrangement. But watching you today, makes me want to help you achieve your desire, and I think it will be fun to help you do it. You can count on me to help you in any way I can."

She left the Salon at five and bought a pair of gym shoes, a pair of shorts, and a plain white shirt. "Now I won't have to wear those horrible starched pants."

She was a tired, but elated woman, when she finally started for home. "I know I'll be able to make my dreams come true now. Everybody wants to help me." The ride was long and dreary, but Sarah flew home on the wings of contentment.

Chapter 6

THE TABLE WAS SET, AND DINNER WAS WAITING FOR HER. SARAH looked in the big pot Dora had simmering on the stove and groaned. The pot was filled with chicken and home-made noodles. "O-h-h-h, I forgot to tell you I couldn't eat stewed chicken, Dora. I wanted to bake it. Well, I'll find something to eat. I'm on a diet and I can't cheat."

"Wha' am I going ta do wit' all this chicken soup an' noodles, Miz Davis?" Dora's forehead was puckered up like a wrinkled old shoe.

"You and Helen can eat it, take some home to Joe."

"Yassum'. Joe'll like that." Joe was Dora's man. Sarah never was sure if he was just her man, or her husband. It didn't matter. He could eat noodle soup either way.

Helen was studying, when Sarah peeked in her daughter's room. "Hi there, book worm, your old mammy's done come home."

She came flying to the door and hugged her mother. "Gosh I thought you'd never get here. What did you do today?"

"Oh lots of things, mostly exercise and massages. I'm so sore I can't stand to touch myself. Come on, honey, let's eat. I'll tell you all about it."

Sarah made herself a fruit salad, sliced some of the white meat from the old hen in the pot; rye crisp crackers, green beans and a glass of tomato juice, completed her dinner. "I don't know how many calories I had today, but I'm sure I didn't go too far off the track tonight. Dora, before you leave I want to tell you what to order for tomorrow, and I want you to fix exactly what I tell you."

Meekly Dora answered from the kitchen door, "Yassum, Miz' Sarah." But she muttered to herself, "She sure actin' funny, so bossy like."

While Dora did the dishes and cleaned up the kitchen, Helen listened to Sarah's recital of the day's happenings. She was a little vague when Helen asked, "But Mother, if you are on a diet, and have exercises, steam baths and massages, it certainly isn't going to take three months to lose thirty pounds." She eyed her mother doubtfully.

"Well, I'm taking lessons in public speaking. You know I've always been so shy about getting up at the P.T.A., and then I'm supposed to speak sometimes at my club, and I'm just too scared. So I thought it might help me to have more poise and courage."

"Gee I think that's grand. What else can you take Mother?"

"Oh they teach everything; dancing, modeling, reducing, treatments, and oh so many things," she finished lamely.

"Is it a school or what?"

"It's an agency I believe. They teach modeling and then place their models. The chorus girls, dancers, jugglers, and tight-rope walkers, pay a monthly fee, like a club or insurance and between engagements they come there to keep in shape and go out on jobs that come in. Oh it's all a big muddle to me. I'm lucky if I find out where and what I'm going to do."

"Gee I'd like to take dancing Mother. Why don't you take it? Daddy likes to dance. He told me so." She watched the changing expressions on her mother's face. "He's never taken you dancing has he Mother?" Sarah shook her head, "I wonder if he goes dancing when he's away from home?"

"That's what I've been wondering for a long time. I'll tell you a secret one of these days. I hope you'll like it." She sounded so mysterious but Helen knew better than to tease about it. "I'm not ready to tell you yet," she explained.

"Mother will you let me take dancing? Then I'll make Ham take it so we can go to the Canteen this winter. The kids have so much fun. It's sort of a club they've organized, to dance and play games and things."

"Yes I know, we discussed it at the meeting, when it was first organized. Your father would throw a fit, if I didn't go with you."

"Well, why couldn't you go? You could learn to dance there. We'd have fun Mother. I'd make Ham dance with you—after he learns of course."

Sarah smiled to herself thinking of the tall Mr. Grayson, who danced divinely, and then Ham, the awkward football player. She might even show Ham a few fancy steps—later on.

Chapter 7

THE NEXT MORNING SHE DRESSED IN HER SHORTS, WITHOUT HER girdle. At nine Mr. Domere came to the ladies room and called her. "Time for gym Mrs. Davis. Are you stiff?" He grinned down at her.

"Am I stiff? Everything in me is crying for help. I don't honestly know if I can do any exercises this morning or not."

"Just take it easy and in a day or so, you won't notice the aches." He walked down the hall with her.

"In a day or so, if I feel like this, I'll probably be dead," Sarah wisecracked.

"Well, I'm glad to see you have a sense of humor."

"I don't have much else do I, Mr. Domere?" She laughed at his quick look. "Oh I heard some of the remarks that got around yesterday. 'The old bag with the money,' 'The dumb cluck' and 'Baggy drawers.' That's why I bought this outfit." She looked down at her slightly bulging shorts.

"Don't let it get you down. You'll make them eat their words one of these days. I'll see you later. Sam is motioning that he's ready." He held the door open for her. And Sarah marched down the long stretch to her pad, feeling naked and self-conscious.

"Okay lady, let's get organized. Got your girdle on?" Sam bellowed.

"No." Sarah yelled back, her face flaming. Everybody roared

with laughter. "How rude can you get?" she flung at him. She didn't have a houseful of teen-agers most of the time, without picking up some of their lingo.

Sam stared at her for a moment, at a loss for words, and then he ordered, "Get set; one—two—three—bend." He kept it up until he was red in the face, nearly all of the class had dropped to the mat long before he called quits.

Sarah jumped rope, played handball, galloped around the room, and tried to use the bars the way Sam showed her, but she couldn't get off the floor. "I said chin yourself, lady, not hang up clothes." He went right on, not waiting for her answer. It might be too much to take. Sarah struggled with the bar for a while and then piled down on her mat. "Let him rave. I'm so tired I could scream." Sam ignored her, evidently sensing that she was at the end of her rope.

When she was leaving for her date with Lil, he came up to her and asked, "Hey lady, do you know how to ride horseback?"

She cringed away from him, "Oh no, I'm afraid of horses."

"Well, wear some blue jeans or pants in the morning, cause you're going to be introduced to a horse."

"Why?" she moaned. Didn't she hurt enough, without not being able to sit down for a week?

" 'Cause you can't lose that extra seat you got by bending. Oh yes, leave that girdle at home. Forget you got it, or throw it away."

"But I've got to wear it. I have to keep my stockings up with it."

"Tie strings around them or something, but no more corsets." Sam strode off, leaving Sarah looking like a lost blimp, losing air.

Lil helped her undress and then closed her up in the steam cabinet. She was so upset over Sam's ultimatum, she didn't feel the heat. She was boiling when Lil put her in there.

"Ah, so it is better this morning. You no care." She looked hopefully at her patient. She rolled Sarah on the table. "This time we try some electric things, to lose fat."

43

Her heavy deft hands, slapped, chopped, dug into Sarah's tender, aching body. "O-h-h-h, I can't stand it. It's killing me. Lil, please don't pound so hard. O-h-h-h." She buried her head in the sheet.

"Lil got to pound, break down fat. You put it on, I got to take it off." She pulled her legs, bent them backwards, massaged her feet. Sarah didn't know whether to laugh or cry.

"Please don't tickle my feet, I can't stand it." Lil pounded with her hands. She reached up and grabbed one of her arms. Sarah fell flat on her face. "You're rougher today than you were yesterday," Sarah complained in a muffled voice.

"You're so soft, I love to work on you." The big Swede took on added inspiration. "Now flop over, we'll work on the top now."

When she finally helped Sarah off the table, she exclaimed, "What's the matter, you limp like a rag." Sarah fell into a chair and folded up.

"Please let me rest a minute, Lil." Lil draped a sheet over her and stood with her hands on her wide hips, surveying the fat figure huddled in the chair. "Okay, I put the belt on you." She held out her hand.

Sarah let herself be propelled towards the big belt hanging down from a motor. "What's that for?" she asked in a quivering voice.

"See I show you." Lil put the belt around her body, and turned the motor on. She looked like she was doing the shimmy in double time. "No hurt, lots of fun. See?" She yelled to Sarah above the noise of the motor.

"Yes I see. Oh well, I guess it can't be any worse than the rest of it. Put it on." She moved over to take Lil's place. Lil snapped the belt on Sarah's white soft hips and then switched the machine on. It seemed that she had suddenly been stuck in an electric mixer. Her teeth chattered, the muscles in her face were having the heebie-jeebies, even her brains rattled. She looked down at her stomach and started to laugh. She laughed so hard the tears ran down her cheeks. Lil came over and turned the motor off.

44

"Oh, lady don't cry, I turn it off." Lil put the sheet back on Sarah and led her to a chair.

"Oh I'm not really crying, Lil, I just happened to see my stomach flapping around and I thought about Santa Claus. When he laughed his belly shook like a bowl full of jelly, remember the old saying?"

Lil scowled at her, nodded her head, and said kindly, "You all right now lady. Get dressed. May is waiting for you."

It was plain that Lil thought Sarah was having hysterics, and wanted to get rid of her.

It was such a blessed relief to go into May's quiet sanctuary, and be anointed with sweet oils. May used the violet ray on Sarah's dry abused skin. She ran the electric rake through her hair. "Gee that feels so good May. Do it again." Sarah begged.

"Too much and too often is not good for your hair or skin. Tomorrow we'll try a mask, and today I'm going to massage some cosmetic oils into your neck, shoulders and arms. You might want to wear an evening dress some night."

Sarah laughed. "I never had one on in my life. I wouldn't know how to act in one."

"Nevertheless, I'm supposed to get you prepared. Do you have any creams or oils at home?"

"No, only a box of powder and a small bottle of perfume," Sarah confessed.

"And your husband doesn't appreciate you? Brother, he should see some of the cosmetic and beauty shop bills I send out every month. He didn't know when he was well off." Her soft hands rubbed the oil into Sarah's plump shoulders.

"I wish you'd give Lil a few lessons in massage. She nearly kills me."

May laughed softly, "That old gal can really dish it out. She is so used to throwing those prize fighters and wrestlers around, that when she gets a hold of something soft, she really puts a dent into it. She gave me a treatment just once. I thought my legs were disconnected from my body. You can have Lil."

"But I don't want her." They both laughed. "She's either

45

going to knock the fat off of me, or pound me into a grease spot."

May paused a moment in her manipulations and informed Sarah, "You should have some creams at home to apply at night, shall I order what you need?"

"Oh please do, I wouldn't know one from another."

"Okay as soon as the salesman comes in, I'll get you a complete beauty treatment, and then I'll show you how to care for your skin." She patted Sarah's fat back. "The skin on your shoulders and back is beautiful, you should wear a strapless gown and show it off."

"Who me? Gee, I wouldn't have the nerve. How would I keep the thing up?"

May giggled, "Well the saying goes, if you have a good foundation it will stay on." She began to remove the creams, "Goodness, it's nearly noon."

Lil stuck her head in the door, "Time for lunch, lady."

Sarah pulled on her blouse and combed her hair. "I just love my next lesson, dancing with Mr. Grayson." She leaned over and said confidentially, "You know if I wasn't a good woman, I could go for him." She blushed at her boldness.

"Well why don't you try being bad for a change, it might be interesting," May advised her.

"Oh no, I'm a married woman. I've been married to George for twenty years," Sarah told her.

"Maybe that's what's wrong with you. It's time for a change." May laughed at her shocked face. "You should know about some married women I know of. They even brag about it."

Mr. Grayson had some dreamy music on the phonograph when she entered their special room. "How's my pupil today. Do you think you'll like dancing," he smiled at her, "with me?"

Sarah took his out-stretched hand and went into his waiting arms. "I love it," she murmured. They didn't say a word until the piece ended. Then he put another record on, and declared:

"You waltz divinely. You've graduated to the fox-trot. Hang on."

46

Sarah became dizzy from the mad whirl. But it was gay, and she was sorry when the hour ended.

Mr. Grayson questioned her, "And you say you never have danced before?" Sarah shook her head. "Strange, you follow me without any effort at all."

"That's because you're such a wonderful teacher, Mr. Grayson."

Domere chuckled from the door, "And you also have a touch of a diplomat in your makeup, Mrs. Davis." He and Grayson exchanged knowing winks. "It's time for your lesson in modeling. Miss Baer is convinced you will be one of her star pupils before long."

"After the fairy godmother touches me with her magic wand, maybe. But now I'm just the ugly duckling." Sarah said it matter-of-factly. She wasn't seeking sympathy.

Grayson observed, "Sometimes beauty of the soul is more important than beauty of the face." He smiled charmingly at Sarah as he left.

"Well what do you know, you've even got Grayson under your spell." Domere went to the desk and got out his memos on Sarah. "Today you learn posture, and posing. I also want Miss Baer to coach you in public speaking. After that, shall we learn to play poker?"

"Oh yes, I've always wanted to gamble. My husband has stag parties and they play poker all night, and I get such a kick out of listening to their talk. Men have all the fun it seems."

"Oh I wouldn't say that, you've just never looked for any. Take your fun when and where you find it." He laughed at Sarah's serious expression, "I believe this plan of yours, will lead you a merry chase."

The hour with Miss Baer passed pleasantly and fast. She was an apt student. Miss Baer found that Sarah need only be told once how to do a thing and it was done perfectly. "You sure catch on fast," she commented.

"I wish Sam thought so. He gets me so confused, I can't tell

47

my left leg from my right. He and Lil drive me crazy." She really didn't mean it.

Her instructor smiled understandingly, "What can you expect from a couple of morons."

The card lesson was very interesting to Sarah. Mr. Domere explained over and over about poker rules and winning hands. "Shall we try a game just to see if you understand?"

"Oh yes, and let's bet some money, to make it real."

He dealt out the cards for a game of five card stud. "But that wouldn't be fair, Mrs. Davis. You might lose."

"What's the difference, don't you know I'm just a poor girl with money?"

They both laughed, and Domere said, "Okay you asked for it. Holler when you're hurt."

The first hand Sarah lost, and by the second, they were betting nickels and dimes. Finally Mr. Domere looked at his watch, "O-h-h-h, it's nearly four o'clock and I've got a novelty man coming to see you, so we'll quit for today."

Sarah made a face. She said disappointedly, "Just when I was catching on. You just look out tomorrow, Mr. Domere, I'll take you to the cleaners."

He put the cards away, and turned to Sarah waiting quietly by the door. "This fellow is going to teach you to play and sing novelty numbers. You know, like Helen Morgan or Ida Lupino. Blues or whatever you can do."

Sarah's clouded blue eyes widened in horror, "I told you I can play, but I can't carry a tune in a basket."

"How do you know you can't? You never tried. You've got so many hidden talents it's time somebody helped you discover them." They had been walking down the hall to Mr. Domere's office. The man he expected was there. He stood up as Sarah entered the room.

"Probably thinks I'm an old lady, and he's been taught to respect his elders," Sarah surmised. Mr. Domere introduced them.

"I want you to find out all you can about this lady's musical background, and see if you can't turn her into a novelty blues

48

singer or something. There's a piano in this next room. You can go in there." He went to the door with them.

"I feel like a guinea pig. I never know what Mr. Domere is going to try on me next."

Jim Fellows laughed at the dumpy woman, "Okay play me a tune, Mrs. Davis. I just want to get an idea, of your rhythm and style."

Sarah sat down at the old upright and played a very staid hymn.

"Don't you know anything modern or classical?" He asked hopefully.

She played a couple of classics. "My daughter plays bop, boogie woogie and jive, but I never tried. I don't know how to start."

So for the next hour, Fellows, clapped hands, sang, played for Sarah and sang with her. She enjoyed it and before the hour was up, she got a faint idea what he was trying to do.

"Well, I guess you'll learn. At least you know music. Your voice is not too bad." He sat and thought for a few minutes, and then decided, "I'll bring you some numbers tomorrow—I believe you can do songs like 'Blue Moon,' 'Stormy Weather,' 'My Man,' and things like that. You've got a low slow voice, we might build you into a real torch singer."

"I don't know why I should have to do this, I'm not going to get up and entertain anybody." Sarah worried all the way home about her singing career.

The next morning Sarah wrapped up a pair of old slacks to take to the gym. "Why should I have to start riding horses at my age. I couldn't sleep all night worrying about it," she muttered to herself as she made a neat package. She wore her flat heeled oxfords, "I suppose I should have boots, but I'm not going to buy a lot of stuff I'll never use again."

Helen wanted to know what she had in the brown bundle, "Oh my old garden slacks. We are going to do some climbing this morning." She lied to her daughter, because she could just imagine how Helen would react. "Oh Mother, I want to learn to ride, please let me!" And so on. Someday she could learn. It

49

might be fun for her, she was young, but Sarah felt her aching back and legs, and wondered how she'd feel after bouncing around on an animal all morning.

In the ladies' lounge she hurried into her slacks, put on an old sweater she had brought along, and went right to the gym. She didn't want Sam to holler at her. It embarrassed her so.

Sam was talking to Mr. Domere when she came in. "We'll be on our way, here's the lady now." He waved to the group that were working out on the different contraptions in the big room. "Come on, let's get going." He herded them into the elevator in the back of the building. An old station wagon was parked alongside the building. "Pile in." Sam opened the door and waited for them to find seats. There were six of them with Sam.

Sarah sat by herself. A man sat in front with Sam, another man sat in the back. Two young girls, probably dancers, Sarah thought, sat together and jabbered like a couple of magpies. No one spoke to her and the trip to the stables was long and full of fearsome thoughts. "It would serve Sam right if I fainted, or fell off, or got hurt." Then she thought of George, "Oh no, I mustn't get hurt, he'd come flying home and spoil everything."

They went to the Million Dollar Bridle Path. Sam went ahead to get their horses. A couple of stable boys brought out two high spirited horses for the two men. Then the girls rode off on two horses that Sarah knew were much too nervous for them to handle. But the four rode off in a swirl of cinders and left Sam standing there with Sarah, to mope along after them. He had a groom bring an old plug out. He looked like he had spent the best years of his life in front of a milk wagon.

The horse cast a wicked glance in Sarah's direction, when she went around to the right side to get on. "Hey, don't you know any better than that, you can't get up on that side. That horse will pulverize you. Come around here." He waited until she wide stepped around the swishing tail. "Whenever you walk behind a horse, speak to him, so he'll know you're back there." Sam spat disgustedly into the dirt. "Remember, always mount a horse on the left side."

50

"Why—I don't see why it should make any difference to the horse, which side I use." Sarah gulped a couple of times and wished she could turn around and run, "I don't wish this poor horse any bad luck, but I wish he'd drop dead," Sarah stalled.

"They got a barn full. Come on now, we've only got an hour." He cupped his hand, Sarah raised her eyebrows at his action. "Stick your itsy bitsy foot in there." Sam had such a sarcastic way of speaking.

Sarah lifted her left foot. "This one?" She asked innocently. He made such a fuss over the left foot.

"Yes this one, unless you want to ride cross legged." He boosted her into the saddle. "Now if you want to go, say giddap. If you want to stop, say whoa. Here's the reins. Hang on to them unless you don't care which way you're going. Now hold your nag here, until I get mine." A boy brought out a beautiful brown horse that towered over Sarah's squatty animal.

"Oh, he's gorgeous. I'd like to ride him after I learn." Sarah gazed at "Raja" as Sam called him, with longing eyes. "I don't think I'd be afraid of him," she confided to Sam.

"Oh no? Well, you just stick to Mr. Dobbin until you learn. You won't have so far to fall." He gave his horse a kick in the ribs and the horse reared straight up in the air and snorted like a train whistle. Old Dobbin pricked up his ears and whinnied.

"Whoa, whoa, o-h-h-h, Sam what's he going to do now?" Sarah's spurt of courage vanished like the dust flying around Raja's impatient hoofs.

"Now I'm no jockey, or authority on horses, but I can ride, and if you will do as I tell you, you can learn. Sit lightly in your saddle, don't hang onto your saddle, hold the reins firmly, but don't saw. Grip the sides of your horse with your knees, and go with the motion of the horse, when he goes up, you go up, when he comes down, you come down. Otherwise you'll look like a bobbing jack rabbit. Got it?" Sarah nodded her head. "Let's go, giddap." He was off before Sarah could say "Giddap." She plodded down the path after Sam—who had stopped and waited for her. He watched her bob up and down on the trotting Dobbin. "Oh my Aunt Fanny, Domere and his bright ideas." He waited until she came up. "What's the matter. Don't you hear very well?"

"There's nothing to hang onto. This saddle isn't equipped with a horn, like some of them in the westerns." Her bangs were standing straight up in the air. The crisp September wind whipped the words out of her mouth.

"Maybe I should have a bell installed too." Sam laughed in a nasty way. "Okay lady, I'll tell you again." He went through his spiel about how she should do it. "Now I'm going on ahead, and then I'll wait for you." He was off like a brown streak.

"Gee I wish I could ride like that. It might be fun, if I wasn't so scared." Sarah told Dobbin, "Come on old fellow, giddap."

The old horse sniffed the air and flung his head up and down, then he started off on a dead run. "Something tells me you've taken the bit between your teeth," Sarah told him. Her teeth chattered from the bumping motion and fear. "Stop, slow down, hey horse what do I say when I want to stop." But the horse kept up his speed. Sarah got a side-ache. She hit the saddle like a ton of bricks. "Must go with the horse, up, down, up, down."

Sam and his horse disappeared around a bend far ahead of them. Sarah couldn't see too well. The wind blew dirt in her eyes, and her scarf whipped across her face, blinding her. She hugged the horse so hard, her legs ached. She held the reins loosely in one hand and the other was hanging onto the front of the saddle for dear life. "They ought to have straps on these things," she grumbled. "Hey horse you're going faster."

And he was. He broke into a stiff-legged gallop, that nearly snapped Sarah's neck off. A piece of paper blew across the road and he shied like a colt, Sarah dropped the reins and hung onto the saddle, terrified. Then it came to her, "Whoa, Whoa," she yelled. The old horse stopped obediently. Sarah made a neat somersault and fell like a rock in the cinders. She had the breath knocked out of her, and then her eyelids flickered open and she could see the horse's feet a couple of inches from her nose. She closed her eyes and moaned faintly, "I'm here, I'm here, don't step on me please." That's the way Sam found her.

"Oh for Pete's sake, maybe I ought to get you a hobby horse. Are you hurt?" He lifted her to her feet and brushed the cinders off her pants.

"Oh don't please, I'm so sore, I can't stand to touch myself. I guess I'm all right." She took a few steps, and announced, "No broken bones, but I'll bet I'll be black and blue." She looked around for her horse. He was grazing peacefully in a grassy patch across the road. "I thought he was going to step on me, but I remembered to tell him I was there."

"Yeah, so you were saying when I got there. Dobbin was way over there in the field." Sam laughed. "Well, shall we get back on?"

Sarah drew back, "Oh no, I'm going to walk back."

"It's a long way lady," Sam warned. She watched him go back after Dobbin. Raja stood near her. . . . Sarah reached out her hand and he jerked his head up and down. "Ugh, you scared me. I was only going to pet you," she whispered under her breath. Sam came back leading her horse. "Okay, I'll help you up." He cupped his hands.

"Must I?" Sarah asked pleadingly.

"You must, unless you want to be laughed at."

"You won't run off and leave me?" Sam agreed. "I wouldn't have fallen if I hadn't forgotten to say whoa."

"Well then how did Dobbin stop?" He grinned, "Now don't try to tell me this scarecrow threw you."

"Oh, I don't know how he did it, but I forgot the word, and he kept going faster and faster, and all at once I remembered the word and I just said it, and plop I hit the dirt."

Sam laughed—Raja blew foam in his face. "That's Raja's way of giving you the horse-laugh, lady. No wonder you fell, don't you know you can't be going at a fast speed and suddenly turn off the power—something has to turn loose. In this case, it was you. I'll bet you you dropped the reins too."

Sarah giggled, "I'll bet I did too. I was too busy hanging on."

53

The horses were walking side by side, Raja side-stepped once in a while like he was dancing, and then old Dobbin would stick his blunt nose over towards the other horse, as if to say, "Don't get too gay big boy." Sarah petted his neck, "He's a nice old fellow, even if he did do me dirty. But I don't want to try it again." She stuck her chin out getting ready for Sam's argument.

But all he said was, "Well you talk it over with Domere. He says you're to ride twice a week. It's a shame you don't want to learn. It's the grandest exercise in the world and after you get the hang of it, you'd love to dash off with the wind in your face and a good horse between your legs." He shrugged as if he didn't care what she did.

They had to wait a few minutes before the others came sweeping up to the barn. Sarah cowered behind Sam as the horses stamped, puffed and jockeyed around the small yard. One of the girls exclaimed, "Gee, there's nothing like a brisk ride to sweep the cobwebs out of your brain." Sam looked at Sarah and smiled.

They were late getting back. Lil gave Sarah a short, but painful rubdown, then a hot shower and she was back in the lounge for her lunch. She was so hungry, she could have eaten three times as much as she did, but she didn't have much time to think about it. Domere came and got her for her dancing lesson. "Well I see you got back in one piece. How do you like your new exercise?"

"I don't. Do I have to learn to ride?"

"If I invested a lot of money in something, I'd want to get all I could out of it. 'Course it's up to you." He watched her expression.

"If you think it's necessary, I'll go," she promised.

"Good girl. If you become a celebrity, don't you think you should know how to ride? Didn't you say your husband liked to ride?" She nodded her head, "Then why don't you take advantage of all the opportunities I'm offering you?" He smiled at her perplexed face.

"I suppose I should, but I can't figure where singing and horse-back riding are going to benefit me."

54

"You never can tell, just be prepared." He opened the door to the room for her dancing lesson. "I hear you're quite a dancer. I'll have to come in and see for myself, one of these days."

"Please do, Mr. Domere. I just love it. And to think I've let all these years go by, without knowing what I was missing." Her voice held a wistful note. "Most of my life."

"Well, now's your chance to make up for lost time. We'll play cards in my office."

The hour she spent dancing flew by. Grayson waltzed with her, fox-trotted, and then showed her the two step. It was amazing how fast she could pick up the steps he taught her. "You'll soon be doing all the new ones, then we'll have a couple of months just to dance. Practice makes perfect."

When she walked into Mr. Domere's office there were several chairs pulled up around the table. "Company?" she asked.

"Yes, I thought it would be more fun if we had some more players, so Sam and May and Grayson are going to join us. You don't mind?"

"Oh no, I think that will be fun. Do you feel lucky today, Mr. Domere?"

"I'm unlucky in love, so I guess I should be lucky in cards. Why?"

"Oh, I just remembered I told you yesterday that I was going to take you to the cleaners." She chose a seat with her back to the light.

"Yes, but remember, we have more people to contend with today. You'll have better gamblers then me to beat. That Sam is a whiz."

"Sam's quite a boy, isn't he?"

Domere laughed as he said, "There isn't much he can't do."

"Except be nice; I think he is about the meanest man I ever ran into. But then I haven't met many, so I'm no judge."

"Don't let May hear you say that. She is absolutely balmy over him."

Grayson came in first, then Sam came in with May. Sarah noticed she was suddenly transformed into a vibrant, scintillating

55

person, so different from the quiet efficient operator, that treated her every morning. "Love can perform miracles," she thought. Maybe that's what she needed. Maybe she was so used to George, he didn't strike a spark in her any more. "Now don't go off the deep end," she warned herself. "I've been a happy, contented married woman for a long time. Nothing has changed, only this wild bee I've got in my bonnet to be pretty. Better leave well enough alone." But her eyes strayed to the handsome face of Bob Grayson, and she couldn't help the teasing thoughts that drifted through her mind. "He might be married, and happily, for all I know." She was glad when Mr. Domere was ready to start the game.

Sarah brought a large stack of chips. Sam asked, "You must figure on losing a lot lady." He grinned impishly at her.

"Don't fool yourself, Sam, she's threatened to take me to the cleaners." Domere's eyes teased her.

"Anything Mrs. Davis does wouldn't surprise me," Grayson added. "If she plays poker like she can dance, look out." Sarah loved his brown eyes. They warmed her, like bright flames.

They played for an hour, Sarah had most of the chips in front of her, she laughed gleefully, "I told you, I'd take you to the cleaners."

Sam growled. "Are you sure you've never played before?"

"Never, not till Mr. Domere showed me how," Sarah vowed.

"If you could ride, like you play poker, you would be famous."

May stood up and cashed in her chips. "I'm broke, besides I have an appointment for a facial. I'll see you." And she left.

Domere looked at his watch, "Yes and Jim Fellows will be coming to give our lady her singing lesson. Better cash your chips in, Mrs. Davis, We'll play tomorrow. Canasta or something." He counted the money out to her. "Thirty dollars winnings."

Sarah stuffed the bills in her bag. "I'm quitting under protest. I'll give you a chance tomorrow to win it back," Sarah promised with a happy smile.

"I'll be here, Mrs. Davis, you'll have to teach me your technique," Grayson drawled in his slow, easy way.

"Now you're teasing me," Sarah told him, "it's just luck. Tomorrow I'll probably lose my shirt."

"Have you ever been to the races, Mrs. Davis?"

"No, but I've heard how exciting they are. That would be a thrill." She clasped her hands like an excited child.

Domere and Grayson laughed at her rapt expression. "We'll have to arrange to go some afternoon, Paul. That would be a good experience for Mrs. Davis, help round out her education," Grayson suggested.

"I guess we could do it. I'll keep it in mind." A buzzer sounded. Thack's voice announced Jim Fellows.

Fellows had brought several pieces. He had Sarah play one of them over and over. "Get some rhythm in you, let yourself go." Sarah tried to get hep, as Helen said, but she was too stiff and afraid. "Do you have a piano at home?" Sarah said yes. "Well get your daughter to show you how she does it. Practice at home. Now come on, get hot."

Fellows beat out the time, Sarah played, and played, finally Fellows pounded the top of the piano with his fist, "Stop, you sound like an old maid in church." He sat down and gave out. He chorded with the left hand and barely touched the keys with his right, but it sounded good. "Now that's the way I want you to play so you can sing to it. Novelty music, your own interpretation of a number. Get a certain way to deliver a song and make it your very own."

"But I don't care for jive or fast music. I might do something with some of the old classics," Sarah promised.

"Practice on one tonight, and let yourself really get in the groove." He looked at her with a quizzical expression, then he shook his head.

"What's the matter, you wanted to ask me something," she stated.

"Yeah. I was going to ask you if you ever drank, but I can see you don't. It might help you to loosen up and act natural." He

57

picked up his hat and the music, "Well do what you can tonight. Rome wasn't built in a day. I'm glad you know how to read the music anyway." He sounded sort of let down.

"It's not too important if I sing or not, so don't worry about it," she consoled him.

"I've got to think about my reputation. I'm the best novelty man on State Street." He left her sitting at the piano.

Sarah's fingers wandered idly over the keys, she started to play an old piece—a favorite of George's, "In the Gloaming" then softly she began to sing. It didn't sound bad, maybe all she needed was to find the right music.

That night Helen was waiting for her Mother when she drove up. "Gee Mother, I've been waiting for hours. Ham wants to take me to the show. May I go please?" she begged.

"Just you and Ham?" Sarah took off her coat and found a soft chair to collapse in.

"No his folks are going to take us to a drive-in. There's such a good picture on." She was combing her hair in front of the hall mirror. "I've had my dinner, I knew you wouldn't mind, seeing you don't eat what I eat." She whirled around and pounced on Sarah, "It seems I never get to see you any more. What did you do that was different today, Mummy?"

"I fell off a—a ladder, for one thing. And I've got to write a speech for my lesson tomorrow, and I have things to do, so I guess you can go to the show." Helen ran to the phone and called Ham. Then, when she finished, Sarah said, "Helen, come here, I want you to show me how you play boogie woogie."

So Sarah and her daughter sat at the piano, until Ham came to get her. "Mother as a jive player, you're a dead beat," Helen went out laughing.

"I am, am I." She tried to copy Helen's lively style, but her fingers just wouldn't move that fast. "Funny, I can type fast."

Dora came in from the kitchen, "Do you all want to eat now Miz Davis?"

"You can get it ready Dora, don't put anything on my plate, that I'm not supposed to have. I'm so hungry, I could eat a horse." Then she remembered, "O-h-h-h, my poor back." She got a pillow and put it on the piano bench. She was picking around on "Honeysuckle Rose" when Dora came cake walking in.

"M-m-m, thass' sumthin'. Play it again, Miz Sarah." She stood there humming, as Sarah played the piece.

"You sing it Dora, and I'll try to play to your voice." Dora had her own inimitable way, but it was arresting. "Why Dora I had no idea you could sing like that. I wonder—" she looked at Dora, contemplating an idea. "I wonder if you could teach me to sing like you do."

"I sure cain try, Miz Sarah. Why for do you want to sing like colored folk?" Dora's black eyes shifted from the music to her employer's calculating face.

"Cause I have to learn to sing in my own individual style, and as long as I'm not doing so well in my language, I'll learn yours."

"Didn't you done told me, that you come frum Alabama?"

"Yes I lived there until I married Mr. Davis. Course I went to a young ladies' finishing school, that tried to erase all my southern accent." She played the piece over softly, trying to capture Dora's catchy swing.

"Well if you bin' in da' south that long, you cain't fa'git it. It's thea' sum' place, Mis Sarah. Le's find it." She began rolling her eyes, and slapping her knee. " 'Honeysuckle Rose,' M-m-m."

Sarah followed along with Dora. They went over the piece until Sarah was able to sing the song alone, almost the same way Dora did it. "He, he, you done got it Miz Sarah, jes' the way the colored folks do it. Don' fa'git to put tha' M-m-m in it." Dora sang a few bars to show Sarah what she meant. Then she exclaimed, "It's nin' clock, Miz Sarah. I gotta git hus'lin, or my Joe will done think I bin cheatin' on him. He's pow'ful jealous o' me, Miz Davis. Is Mistah Jawge jealous o' you?"

Sarah laughed at Dora's intense look, "N-o-o-o, Mistah Jawge nevah worries about his po' ole' Sarah."

Dora clapped her hands gleefully, "See deah! yo' done say it lak' I do!"

59

After Dora had gone, Sarah ate her cold, meager supper and actually enjoyed it. She could have eaten more; but there were other things more important than food. She was anxious to get back to the piano. She was as excited and eager as a child. "Why," she thought, "I haven't been this interested in anything in a long time." Besides, she had a big idea—a tremendous one. If she really looked different at the end of her course, she could fool George completely—with a southern accent. He always frowned on her "Alabama brogue" as he called it; he said it sounded so affected. He might like it from some honey pot he didn't know. The idea was so alluring that she decided then and there to have the surgery and the face-lifting done.

Before she went back to the piano, she poured herself a shot of whiskey and squirted some seltzer water in the glass. She sipped on it, and made a face, she added some more water, sipped some more. It wasn't bad, maybe, but she didn't exactly like it. She sipped some more as she went over "Honeysuckle Rose." She became so engrossed in mocking Dora's way of singing that she drank her highball without realizing it was gone. When she reached for the glass and there was no more liquor in it, she giggled a little. Well, maybe she could really cut loose now. She banged away on the piano and drawled out "Honeysuckle Rose" in Dora's best delivery, memorizing every little lazy note Dora put in it, until she sounded like an old Negro mammy singing to some little tyke.

The door bell rang and Sarah's hands dropped to her lap, guiltily, almost. It must be Helen. Suppose she heard her, suppose she smelled the liquor? Sarah walked to the door slowly. Helen came bouncing in and looked down at the radio.

"Mother, why did you turn it off?"

"Turn what off, dear?" Sarah hoped she sounded innocent.

"The radio, of course! There was the most tantalizing singer on. Didn't you hear her?" She was incredulous. "No honey, I must have been in the bedroom." Sarah felt even guiltier about the lie.

"I wonder what station she came in on." Helen switched the set on, dialed here and there. "She's gone."

"Was she really good, dear?" Sarah asked, just to hear what Helen's comment would be.

"Was she good! I stood by the door for a few seconds before I rang, just listening to her. She hit me, hard."

When Helen went to hang up her coat, Sarah ran over to the piano for the highball glass. She sneaked to the kitchen; she felt like a thief in the night as she washed the glass and put it away.

Helen had trailed her. "I'm beat, Mummy, I'm going to bed." Sarah turned her head and prayed that Helen would not smell the liquor. She hugged her daughter tight for a moment and then gave her a quick kiss on the top of her head.

"Good night, dear. I hope you'll forgive me for leaving you alone so much, but just think, Helen, for the first time in my life, I'm having fun!" What a confession to make to your daughter. But how good to have a daughter you could say it to.

"I don't mind with Dora here, but I do miss you. It takes you so long to get home."

It was late by the time Sarah had written a speech for her public speaking lesson. "So many irons in the fire, it's getting me down," she thought. But it was fun—more than fun, it was glorious to have those irons in the fire even if she did quake sometimes over the future, and her wisdom.

A hot bath relaxed her a little, but her body was so sore, it felt like a boil. "I'll bet I won't be able to walk in the morning."

She had nightmares all night about Raja running away with her. Twice she woke up screaming for Sam. "Ugh! Why can't I dream about Bob," she thought, half-amused at the idea, halfway really wanting to. Sleepily she wondered what George would think if he heard her screaming for Sam. She'd have to be careful, "Careful of what?" Bob asked as he took her in his arms; they danced until dawn. Sarah woke up with Helen standing over her.

"I've been shaking you for a long time. You must have been unconscious."

"M-m-m, I was in heaven," she murmured still half asleep. Then she moved, "O-h-h-h, my back!" She tried to sit up. "I must have hurt it when I—when I fell. I don't think I can get up."

Helen put her arm around her and helped her to get to the edge of the bed. "Why don't you call Mr. Domere, and be excused today, Mummy?"

"No, I'll take a hot shower, that'll help." Helen helped her limp into the bathroom. It was agony even to lift her leg to get into the tub. Sarah gritted her teeth and turned on the water as hot as she could stand it. When at last she dried herself and looked in the mirror at her back, there was nothing black and blue to see. Maybe the bruise didn't show, but she could feel it. Oh, how she could feel it. She dressed slowly, painfully, and hobbled out to the breakfast table. Helen was nearly finished.

"Mother, you look terrible! You'd better stay home, honest! Why do you walk spraddle-legged?"

"Because I hurt!" Sarah hastened to say, afraid Helen might guess about the horseback riding. "I'm lucky I can walk at all." Sarah poured some coffee. "Did you eat enough breakfast?" Looking at Helen's fresh, healthy and shining face, she added, "If I was as pretty as my daughter, I wouldn't have to suffer so." She eased herself into the hard kitchen chair, and the bruised muscles hurt so sharply that tears came into her mild blue eyes.

"Mother, you can't go down there the way you look and act. What would Daddy say?" Helen was worried.

Sarah frowned and said sharply, "You mustn't breathe a word of this to him. We must pretend everything is going along just like always. Promise."

"Well, I won't tell him anything if you don't want me to, but I think you're foolish to go through all this agony. We'll love you just the same, Mother. You don't have to change."

Sarah's heart was tender. Bless the girl. George would agree on the foolishness, but would he on the love?

"I'll be all right, dear, don't worry about me. I'll have tomorrow and Sunday to rest up. Now you'd better hurry."

When Dora came Sarah swore her to secrecy too. "I want to

surprise Helen and Mister George, so we'll practice when there's no one here and then some night I'll put on a show." Dora grinned, delighted to be part of the conspiracy. Sarah drummed her fingers on the table thinking. Finally she asked, "Dora, can't you arrange to stay all week? It's so late when you go home. You could have Saturday and Sunday off." She looked hopefully at the mild black face.

"No'm, that Joe o'mine, he'd be out lookin' fo' another woman. I just bettah go along home." A good man was hard to find, and Dora was going to hang onto hers.

Sarah laughed and gave in. "Okay Dora; I never thought about that angle."

Dora wagged her head. "When yo' have a man like Joe, yo' got to figure all the angles."

It was Friday, and after the Chamber of Horrors, which Sarah mentally daubed Lil's corner, she ate her lonely lunch and then lay down on one of the lounges to rest. For the first time she did not look forward to her dancing lesson.

Jill came in and spoke to her. "You poor thing, I'll bet this has just about got you licked. How are you doing?" She sat down and lit a cigarette.

"I'll be all right when I can get over all these aches and pains. Lil says I never used any of my muscles before, and I'm inclined to believe her." Sarah was surprised to see real sympathy in the girl's face.

"It's a pretty rough life, no matter what you do. If I don't keep in shape, I don't get a job. If I don't get a job I can't eat."

"Isn't there anything you can do, besides dancing?" Sarah asked.

"Never learned to do anything much in school, so now I'm paying for it. Then my lip kills my chances sometimes. I could really hit big time if I had it fixed. I know I could."

"Why don't you save a little at a time and have it done?"

"I never got the habit; money and I are soon parted. It isn't so easy to save these days." She had her shoes off, rubbing her toes again.

63

"I imagine dancing is hard on your feet," Sarah ventured.

"Are you kidding?" I bet they've danced a million miles, and they feel like it. Cheap shoes don't help any." She puffed awhile and blew the smoke towards the ceiling, then gave a short laugh. "One of these days I'll find an old guy with dough and then I'll be all set." She ground her cigarette out and patted Sarah's bare knee. "Keep your chin up; I admire your spunk."

She went to the door. "Not every woman would have the guts to do what you're doing."

Sarah wanly smiled her thanks and hoped Helen wouldn't ever have to know Jill's sort of life. "Poor kid, I'll bet she isn't twenty yet, and so bitter and hard."

The dancing lesson turned out better than Sarah had expected. She told Mr. Grayson just how battered she felt, and he was most considerate. He took most of the hour to demonstrate for her some of the steps she was to learn. Rumba, samba, bolero, mombo, even jitter-bug. He was so graceful he was a joy to watch—though she would rather be in his arms—and suave, even in his dancing. Sarah felt her heart jump as he smiled at her. They danced a waltz and a slow fox-trot and then he gave her a brief lesson in the two step. Too bad she couldn't dance the fat off.

Time always sped by whenever she was with him. She sighed, "Why is it the things you enjoy never last long enough?" And thought, "He'll think I'm a silly fool."

An amused chuckle made her look up at him. "That's why we enjoy them; if we were to glut ourselves on pleasures, then they would cease to be pleasures."

"I guess you're right, but I've never had many pleasures and I guess I'm just greedy."

Bob Grayson said seriously, "I haven't had too many myself. You have a lovely daughter, a fine home. I'm just an orphan, no relatives, no family; just a hotel room for a home." He opened the door, waited for Sarah to precede him, then he added, "Of course I have my career, and I have my moments." He smiled down on her with those warm brown eyes. Everything about him wove a spell, and it would be so easy to fall completely under it.

Mentally she shook herself and changed the subject. "Are you prepared to be beaten today, Mr. Grayson? I'm going to take all you've got. I can feel it in my bones."

And she did. After an hour's playing, Sarah had to quit for her singing lesson, and she had won fifty dollars. "Gee, you sure can win or lose fast in a poker game, can't you?" she asked the four long faces around her.

Sam grunted, "Are you sure you never played poker before?"

Sarah crossed her heart, "Cross my heart Sam, I didn't know a spade from a club."

He looked at Domere, "Do you have a class open wherefore you could teach me the art of card playing?"

Everybody laughed, but Sarah knew Sam and May could gladly cut her throat. Grayson she didn't think cared; it was all in fun to him. Mr. Domere assured her that she had won it fairly and squarely.

"Do you have a horseshoe with you?" Sam asked sarcastically.

"Should I?" Sarah was all innocence.

"Oh, brother, I give up and bow to the lady." He joined in the laugh that went around the table.

"I go, but I'll be back," Sarah warned them.

Sam muttered, "Who says that dame is a dumb cluck?"

"It's amazing what a little general knowledge will do for some people," Domere remarked, as the door closed on Sarah.

Out in the hall she met Dr. Bloom and he reached out and grabbed the handful of bills she was holding. "What's this, giving away money?"

Sarah laughed and confessed, "I took it away from some card sharks." Looking at the money, she impulsively asked, "How much would you charge to fix a small harelip?"

The doctor rubbed his chin thoughtfully, "A small one? You wouldn't have a little girl by the name of Jill in mind, would you?"

Sarah nodded her head, seriously. "I feel sorry for her."

"Well, I wouldn't charge too much for it."

"Here, fifty dollars." Sarah counted out the money she'd won. "Take this on account. Give her the operation, and bill me for it. It will give Jill so much satisfaction; besides, I'll win this money back on Monday. Why don't you play with us?"

"What, and have you take all my money too?" The doctor had a look of horror on his face.

"There's always the possibility you'll beat me," she smiled and left him standing there with the fifty in his hand.

"It's a good thing there's a few people around like her," the doctor thought as he watched Sarah's plump, short figure disappear in the next room. "At least her heart's all right."

Fellows, waiting in the little music room, was in for a surprise. Sarah's eyes were dancing when she sat down to the piano and began to sing. "Honeysuckle Rose" lilted softly through the room. Fellows listened for a few minutes, then he slipped out of the door and got Domere. "Come in here. Did you ever hear anything like this?"

The two men looked at each other, Domere's eyebrows sky-high and Fellows grinning broadly. "Most amazing person I've ever met," Domere whispered.

"She'll be a sensation." Fellows strode over to the piano. "How did you do it, Mrs. Davis? I knew you had it in you, you just never found the right track." He patted her shoulder. "Over the week-end, learn another one. If you can do all your songs with the interpretation you're using—" He ran his fingers through his hair. "I don't know how to class you. You're not a blues singer, not strictly. Not a torch singer; but will you wow them!" He looked at her several times as if he couldn't believe his ears.

Chapter 8

IT WAS ALMOST SEVEN-THIRTY WHEN SARAH ARRIVED HOME. HELEN met her at the door. "Oh, Mother! Daddy's called, and he's going to call back real soon. Gee, I thought you wouldn't get here, and I didn't know what to tell him." She followed her Mother to the bedroom.

Sarah hung up her coat, put on her old bedroom slippers and smoothed her hair, as Helen talked. "Don't get so upset, dear. You could just tell him I went shopping or something." She eased down on the vanity stool.

She had picked up the box of creams, lotions and oils May had ordered for her. Now she unwrapped the packages and lined them up on the vanity. Bottles, jars and boxes. Helen smelled and sampled. "O-h-h, what are you going to start now, a beauty shop?"

"No, this is a home beauty treatment. I'll show you how to use some of them if you want me to." She cleaned her face with the cleansing cream. "Of course, you only need protective care, you don't have to rejuvenate your skin as I do." She cleaned out a bottom drawer. "I'll hide them in here, so your father won't see them."

"Mother, you never did that before; hide things, tell stories!" Helen's eyes regarded her Mother mischievously.

"There's a lot of things I never did before." She hadn't meant

67

it to sound mysterious, but she felt secretly pleased when it did.

Then the phone rang.

"Sarah?" George always shouted on the phone.

"Yes, George. Sorry I missed you before. I was down in the Loop."

"H-m-m-p, well, I thought I better call tonight. I have a conference on tomorrow night, I'll probably be tied up till late. How have you been?"

"Fine, and you?" she asked dutifully.

"I'm okay, Sarah. Well, this thing costs money, so I guess I better hang up. If you need me just call the office. They can put their finger on me any time. I'll call you next week."

"All right, George, be careful." That was all. Sarah limped out to the kitchen.

Dora had her supper ready; each night it looked smaller and smaller. "Are you sure you didn't forget something, Dora?" Sarah checked the menu.

"No'm, I done put it all on there. But I sure undahstand how yo' feel. Why, I give my bird more'n yo' eat, Miz Sarah." She cackled as she moved around the kitchen. "I'm sure glad Joe like 'em fat." Then she added darkly, "Trouble with him, he like 'em skinny too."

Sarah ate slowly to make the food last longer, but she couldn't fool her stomach; it was still hungry. "My stomach thinks my throat is cut. I don't mind while I'm at school, but when I have time to think about it, I nearly starve to death."

Dora moved her big hulk close to Sarah, "Did yo' sing, Miz Sarah? Like I showed yo'?" Her face beamed, her voice was a stentorian whisper.

"M-m-m, I did, Dora! And I wowed him." They giggled over their secret. Sarah put her finger to her lips. "S-h-h-h." She pointed to the other room and Dora nodded her head understandingly.

The phone rang again. Sarah heard Helen talking on and on.

"It must be Ham. That boy is really gone over Helen."

68

"Yessum, he done called three times already," Dora informed her.

"Oh no! No wonder George sounded peeved; I'll bet our line was busy all evening."

Helen stuck her head in the kitchen. "Mum, I'm going across the street to Betty Ann's. I won't be gone long."

That could be taken advantage of. Sarah hurried to the piano. Dora came in, dish towel dangling in one hand. "Yo' know, Miz Sarah, I been thinkin' 'Pickaninny Baby' is a song fo' yo.'"

"I believe I have it." Sarah stood up and dug through the piano bench. "Here it is; sort of tattered and torn. It must be thirty years old." She ran through it, then turning to Dora, she said, "Okay, Dora, beat it out."

If George could have peeked in, he would have seen their maid swinging the dish towel, slapping her hips, and singing. Sarah joined in, and before Helen came back, she had a good idea of Dora's version of the song. "I'm going to build up a repertoire, Dora, and one of these days, I'll break loose."

"Oh, Lordy, that'll be somethin'." Dora went swinging back to the kitchen.

Wanting to be secretive about this even with Helen, Sarah couldn't practice on a week-end. Helen usually stayed home on Saturdays getting her clothes in order for the coming week, and fixing her nails and hair. "Yet I've got to practice," Sarah thought. She lay awake hours that night before she hit on a bright idea.

Saturday morning, she crawled out of bed and went through the motions of getting breakfast, but her body felt numb and her brain dead. She had an empty void in her stomach. All she could think of was food. She carefully followed her own menu, but she suffered as she looked at Helen's plate of eggs and bacon and toast covered with butter and delicious jam. "For heaven's sake, come here and get your breakfast, before I lose my nerve."

Helen came to the table laughing, "Poor Mother, you deserve a lot of credit for your determination. How much have you lost?"

"I don't know, I haven't weighed myself. I thought I'd wait

until Tuesday morning. That will be a week." She was all through her meal while Helen was still leisurely munching on her toast. "Forgive me, dear, but I'll have to be excused. It's more than I can stand." Sarah left the room.

She went to the phone and rang a dance studio in their neighborhood, and she made an appointment for Helen at one o'clock. That would give Sarah an hour to herself. It wasn't that she wanted to get rid of her sweet child, it was just that there were a few things she would have to learn by herself; how to drink and smoke, for example, as well as sing like an Alabama girl.

Helen was delirious with joy when her mother told her. "I'm going to make Ham take them too. Every man should know how to dance. He thinks that old football is the most important thing in his life."

When Sarah drove Helen to the dancing lesson that afternoon, she stopped on the way back and bought herself a pack of cigarettes, king-size; they looked so smart when other women smoked them.

At home she mixed herself a highball, then went over her two numbers. "Boy, I'm really living," she whispered to her reflection in the mirror as she danced by, pretending the handsome and suave Mr. Grayson was there with her. "Shall we try a two step, Mr. Grayson?" She laughed softly, and she felt like a foolish old dog trying to learn new tricks. George would be ashamed of her. She supposed she ought to be ashamed of herself, but at least her body didn't hurt quite so badly and her stomach had quit gnawing. "No wonder people drink," she thought. "It sort of puts a different light on things." She guessed she might be the least bit tight.

She grew tired of dancing around the room by herself, so she sat down with the cigarettes. "Now I'll learn to smoke like the rest of them do it." She lit the long cigarette, held it loosely in her short fingers, and took a long drag. It almost knocked her out. She coughed until the tears ran down her cheeks. She would have to be more cautious. Next she took a quick puff, letting the smoke out quickly, like Jill had done. This time she didn't choke, she tried it again. "H-m-m, simple when you know how," she told herself.

After Helen's dancing lesson, they went for the groceries, a steak for her daughter, and a lamb chop for herself. Sarah had to carry her menu along, so she wouldn't slip up through ignorance. At the bakery counter, Sarah stood and drooled over all the whipped cream cakes, pastries and pies.

"Buy some cream puffs, Mother. Ham might come over tonight and we can have a snack."

Ham was there bright and early, as usual. Helen raved to him about her dancing lesson and the teacher, who was "dreamy." Sarah heard her tell Ham, "Next week you're going, too, I made an appointment for you."

"I have to practice, Helen, you know that! Besides—" he hesitated at the stubborn look on Helen's face, "I don't care about dancing."

"Oh you don't care about it! Well, let me tell you Ham Mooney, I'm not going to be the only wallflower in the crowd. You'll go or I'm not going out with you any more."

In a few minutes Sarah heard the front door open and close. She peeked in the living room and Helen was glaring at the door. "Go and don't ever come back, you big dope." She was sputtering all to herself with anger.

"Why, Helen, I'm surprised at you. Poor Ham, I feel sorry for him."

Helen even glared at Sarah. "Well, you can rest assured that no man is going to treat me the way Daddy's always treated you. Sit at home and suck your thumb! Not me!" She dashed to the phone, and soon she was talking to somebody by the name of Jack. Honey couldn't be sweeter, thought Sarah, as she listened to her daughter's line. She came flouncing back into the room. "Jack's coming over, and Betty Ann and Tommy Myers are coming in to work on a musical act we're going to put on for the next P.T.A. meeting."

Sarah sighed guiltily. She had forgotten the meeting on Wednesday. She would have to miss quite a few. "Maybe you had

71

better tell Mrs. Samuels that I'm taking treatments, and I won't be there until the first of the year."

"She asked where you were the other day, and I said you had an appointment. What kind of treatments shall I say, Mother?" Helen was preoccupied. Probably working poor Ham over in her mind, Sarah surmised.

"Oh, you needn't go into it, dentist or neurotic, or something like that. Tell her I'm being treated by psychotherapy." Sarah smiled. She could just see the look of horror on Mrs. Samuel's face.

"Mother, you're a mess, what does that mean?"

"Oh, it's a mental and spiritual healing. In a way that's what I am doing, only it's physical. But it helps the mental—it really does." Helen grinned in understanding.

When Helen's company came, Sarah disappeared into her room. She took a long luxurious bath, then she tried all her creams. She smelled like a flower garden. She had never used creams before, and now she didn't think she'd ever let herself be without them. They made her feel so cared for, so pampered. She rubbed cream everywhere she could reach. With this as with the dancing, maybe with everything, it was just as she had told Bob, "There's so much I've missed, I'm greedy."

Later she went to the kitchen and fixed the kids a snack, hot chocolate and cream puffs. Surely they wouldn't eat three apiece. She stood there a long time, looking at the cream puffs. Well, Helen wouldn't eat three, anyway. Sarah gave in to temptation. She relished every morsel of the creamy pastry. Then she looked on the chart: "Cream puff, small, with whipped cream——three hundred calories." Oh dear, her finger traced down the list: "Whiskey, mixed drink——two hundred and fifteen calories." "Oh, I didn't know liquor contained calories." What could she do on the morrow to work off those five hundred calories?

Chapter 9

THE SECOND WEEK FLEW BY AND SARAH PROGRESSED BEYOND HER expectations. She could really dance; she was graceful and gay and carefree. No complexes, no restrictions; she forgot she was plain and unloved. Everyone at the school was kind and helpful. Miss Baer enjoyed coaching her "star pupil" as much as Sarah enjoyed learning the art of modeling, and the secrets of public speaking. And Sarah had more confidence in herself, she wasn't afraid of old Dobbin when Sam took her riding. Fellows kept urging her on to learn new pieces, and his praise warmed Sarah's heart, especially the day he told her, "As soon as you master several songs, I'll find a spot for you to show."

The worst moment came when Lil weighed her and she hadn't lost an ounce. She nearly cried from frustration. "I ate one cream puff, and to think that all the abuse I've taken hasn't made any difference."

Lil marked down one hundred and fifty-five pounds. "When you cheat the scale knows. One cream puff, and what else?"

"Nothing—except two highballs." Then she defended herself. "I'm supposed to learn how to smoke and drink."

She learned other card games that second week. Domere had laughed and said, "Everybody's too broke to play poker this week, so we'll play something else for the fun of it."

On Friday, he asked if Sarah would like to go to the race track.

73

"If we're going to teach you how to bet on the ponies, we'd better do it today. The season will soon be over. Be ready right after lunch."

As soon as she finished her miserable few calories, she dressed in her old black suit, pulled her prim little black hat to a jaunty angle, and grabbed up her top coat. Lil came in for the tray and stood back as Sarah dashed through the door. "I'm off to the races, Lil!" She was thrilled to the tips of her flat heeled oxfords.

Sam drove the school's big limousine, with May and Domere in the front, and in the big back seat, Sarah and Bob Grayson. Sarah felt like a school girl on her first date.

The air was crisp and tangy—a wonderful day for the races. Grayson smiled at the little woman's exuberance. "It makes me feel ten years younger just watching you. Do you feel lucky?"

"Oh yes, I'm so happy I must be lucky."

Once there they all huddled over the racing forms and tip sheets, Sarah with a hundred questions on her lips. They had a few minutes to make their daily double bet, and Mr. Grayson, trying to be helpful said:

"Now according to the consensus, in the first race they pick Old Sal to win, in the second, Mr. Big. You play them together for the daily double."

He jotted down his selections and handed Sam his bets, and a ten dollar bill.

"I think I'll just bet one to win," Sarah said. She read the names of the horses before she handed Sam a ten dollar bill. "I'll play Gay Dora to win."

Sam looked at the horse: number seven, five to one. "No one gives that dog a peep. Why did you pick that one?" She didn't have a chance, but Sam was curious.

"Oh, my cook is named Dora, and sometimes she gets pretty gay." Sarah laughed at the blank look that came over Sam's face.

Gay Dora won. That was the beginning of what was for Sarah a thrilling afternoon, and for the others, a weird one.

In the second race, she liked Star Fairy because the jockey's

74

name was George. Star Fairy didn't have a chance in a whirl-wind, but Star Fairy won.

Sarah was delighted to see a horse named Pretty Helen in the third race. By the time the bets were collected on that one, Sam was crying to May, "What's the use? I stay up all night studying the records. I study the time, the blood lines, the owners, and the jockeys and the averages. And I can't hit an even money favorite, and here some dame comes along and wins a hat full, just because her old man's name is George or something."

May said, matter-of-factly, "So what's going to keep you from playing her picks?"

The next race all of them listened to Sarah's calm assertion, "I want to play number five, John's Pride."

Sam still couldn't help being scornful. "Why do you like him? He's a long shot, twenty to one. Nobody likes him. I suppose your daughter's boy friend's named John?"

Sarah smiled as she watched the horses parading to the post. "No, that's Ham. John's Pride has such a long pretty tail."

Domere smiled, "I'll chance a little," he said, and gave Sam two dollars to bet on Sarah's horse. But he put twenty dollars on a favorite. Bob Grayson risked two on Sarah's choice, too, so Sam shrugged and went along with them. "The long pretty tail it is," he said, "but only for two bucks."

John's Pride came through with his tail flying. He won going away. Sarah was happy, but not surprised. "He had as good a chance as any in the race," she declared.

Sam swore. "My first winner in a month; and I only play two dollars! Stand up, lady, I want to see something."

Sarah stood up, wondering.

"No, sit down." He shook his head. "I thought maybe you were sitting on a horseshoe."

"Should I be?"

"Oh, for Pete's sake. Forget it and pick another horse!"

Sarah was very late getting home that night, but her purse was crammed with bills, and she was smiling less at her luck than at Sam's attitude. "Why don't you find a job as black jack dealer for the lady? I never saw anything like it. I swear to **God**, never in my life! Cards, horses!!" He was convinced that Sarah was a "natural."

George called before Sarah had been in the house five minutes. She was a little breathless and so happy she could hardly talk. It took several minutes to convey to George that absolutely nothing was wrong.

Chapter 10

SUDDENLY SARAH HAD LOST SEVEN POUNDS AND HER STOMACH HAD shrunk. She blessed the day, for she wasn't tempted to cheat on her diet any more. She was doing splendidly in every class. She and Dora practiced together every chance they could get, and Sarah had perfected several more songs. Vainly she thought that her voice might be the gold mine in the back yard. George called on a Friday evening. Sarah should meet him at the airport early Saturday morning.

"Oh why can't he take a cab? I'm so tired I can't see straight."

But she went, wearing dark powder to cover up her peeled, bleached, and improved complexion. She wore a heavy suit and her fur coat. She would have to wear a lot of clothes while George was home.

His visit was short, pleasant and uneventful. Sarah breathed a sigh of relief as she noticed his complete unawareness. To him, nothing unusual was taking place.

He crabbed a bit about Helen taking dancing lessons. "Why didn't you ask your old Dad to show you how to trip the light fantastic?"

"Why, Daddy, you never go to a dance. I thought you had forgotten how."

He looked startled—Sarah wondered if it were a guilty look as well, but he offered his daughter no further argument.

77

He did notice that Sarah's meals were different from his and Helen's. "If you've been starving yourself while I've been gone," he remarked, "you might as well quit. You're still as fat as ever."

Sarah smiled a smug little smile, and devoted herself to making him comfortable—as long as she couldn't practice her music.

When he left early Monday morning, she persuaded him to take a cab, so she could get Helen off to school. He'd have to get over this business of being spoiled.

That was the day that brought Sarah a tremendous surprise. Fellows had found a spot for her on a radio program featuring a contest. Afraid she would turn it down because of her shyness, he had already approached the sponsor of the program, and they had worked out a scheme to get Sarah to sing without being seen or having contact with anyone besides Fellows.

But before he told her he asked, "Mrs. Davis, do you think you can learn about twenty songs within this month?"

"Oh yes! I must know ten now, and it's getting easier for me to get the hang of it. Why?" Sarah liked Fellows and felt perfectly at ease with him or performing for him.

"Well, I've found something just made to order for you. A mystery program. You will sing two songs a day. No one but me will see you or talk to you. You'll have your audition in a room with the piano, the mike, and me. You don't have to be afraid that anyone will see you, or know who you are." He talked hard, for he felt he had to convince her.

"What sort of program is it?" Sarah's heart was doing double time. Singing on the radio!

"The Banner Soap Company is putting it on for a month. For so many wrappers, and a description of the mystery singer, they can win all sorts of prizes, from money to clocks, dolls, bicycles and so on. The one guessing your weight, age, looks and so on, will be the winner, and of course, the winner has to send in the most soap wrappers." He smiled at her doubting face.

"Do you think I'm good enough to sing over the air?"

"You're a sensation, and I ought to know. I've been grooming novelty and specialty singers for a long time now."

"I'd have to go under a fictitious name, and no one must see me because I'm going to look a lot different a month from now." Sarah's mild blue eyes regarded Fellows earnestly. "Will you promise me that I will not be subject to any publicity at all?"

"I give you my word of honor, Mrs. Davis. I'll bring you the contract to sign, I'll go to the studio, stay with you while you sing and bring you home without anyone getting close to you. Is it a deal?"

"Could I wear a veil?"

He looked as if he thought that was carrying shyness a little far, but he nodded his head. "You can dress any way you like." He got up and walked over to the piano, and looked down at the plain little woman sitting there with her hands on the piano keys. "You will receive one hundred dollars a week for four weeks, starting the third week of November and ending the third week of December. Of course you understand I'll get a percentage for my fee." He smiled disarmingly at her.

Sarah waved the statement away. It wasn't the money that was exciting. He could have it all if he liked. "I'm going to sing on the radio, me, Sarah Davis, the radio." She said the words softly, not quite believing it. Maybe Helen would get to hear the singer she wanted to find the other night, after all.

Sarah moved through all her daily tasks, lessons and moments of fun, in a detached way. The contest was a deep dark secret and she couldn't confide in anyone, not Helen, not even Dora, who helped make it possible. She still won at poker, absentmindedly stuffed the money in her purse, smiled at Sam's barbs, and went on her quiet way.

Sam told Domere and Grayson after a losing poker session, "You know I've come to the conclusion that our little lady is nuts."

From then on Sarah arranged all sorts of outings with Ham, to get Helen out of the house every evening for an hour or so, so that she could practice. Ham was agreeable: his love, money to spend on her, and her mother's permission besides. Sarah's price was secrecy and it all worked out beautifully.

79

Meanwhile Sarah had lost twenty pounds and had to buy several skirts and blouses to wear to the school. She felt better and looked much better.

Then George came home on his monthly visit and the week end was a nightmare. She managed to pad herself with three or four undergarments under voluminous house dresses and wrappers. Camouflaging her face was harder, for May's efforts had brought a fresh, pink-tinged bloom to Sarah's once sallow, rough skin. She felt blooming inside, too, and so every word she said, every move she made had to be closely watched.

It was a heavy strain on Sarah, having George scrutinize her features across the table, or make love to her in his clumsy way. But he was so used to his little brown wren that he just took it for granted nothing had changed. That was a relief, but it did infuriate her. Well, he wouldn't take her for granted again. Not after his next visit. That was planned for the Christmas holidays, and George Davis was going to get the surprise gift of his life.

Chapter 11

THE FIRST WEEK SARAH HAD BEEN SINGING OVER THE RADIO, HELEN had been absorbed in a school play for the holidays. Sarah wanted to let her know indirectly about the four o'clock program, but was afraid to draw her attention to it for fear she might get suspicious. Helen said, wrinkling up her brows one night, "Mother, where do you suppose Ham is getting all the money for sodas and square dancing and everything he takes me to?" Sarah played innocent. There was so much pretending to do!

The papers had been carrying notices of the contest, and one evening there was a small write-up of the mystery singer, a complimentary write-up about the "voice with an unusual delivery."

Sarah's face flushed with happiness, and she casually drew Helen's attention to the article. "Have you heard this mystery singer, honey? We heard her today and I'd say she was a colored woman. She has sort of a cute voice."

Helen took the paper and read the contest rules and the write-up. "This might be fun. I think I'd like to try. Can I order some Banner Soap, Mother?"

The next night Helen met Sarah with a hug and an exclamation. "It's her, Mother. The one I heard that night you turned the radio off." She danced around the room. "She's wonderful. She haunts me for some reason, as though I've known her a long time. Her voice just makes me shiver inside." She dashed to the piano and tried to imitate the voice she had heard.

Dora stuck her head around the door and grinned broadly at Sarah.

"Wen' ev'a yo' is ready Miz Sarah, I is too."

Sarah hummed softly to herself. So Dora knew. She'd have to bribe her.

In the kitchen Dora sat Sarah's food on the table and whispered in her ear, "I almos' drap the 'tatoes when I hears that 'M-m-m-m' comin' ovah the radio. I says to myself it's Miz Sarah, sure as I'm bo'n. I keep my mouf shet." Her old black face beamed with pride and loyalty. "I won' tell a soul," she promised Sarah faithfully, hand over heart.

"Will this help you to hold your tongue, Dora?" Sarah laid twenty dollars on the table.

"O-h-h Lordy, will it Miz Sarah, for that, I'd be deef and dumb." She showed all her white teeth as she scooped the money up and jammed it into her apron pocket.

"If you'll just keep our secret until the middle of next month, I'll give you some more." Then Sarah's face took on a stern expression. "If you tell, we can both go to jail. Don't tell a soul, not even Joe."

"I'll sew my mouth shut," Dora declared.

The week-end was Sarah's, with no program to sing for. Dora came the two extra days to help her and Ham obligingly took Helen to the movies two days in a row.

The second week of the contest, Fellows brought to the school several letters addressed to the Mystery Singer. Two were requests for a repetition of "Honeysuckle Rose" and three wanted her to speak a few words each day. The station liked both ideas, and so the Mystery Singer was allowed two minutes daily, after her songs, to say a few words to the listeners. Jim Fellows helped her plan it, and both of them were delighted as Sarah's voice dripped with southern sweetness.

Helen was excited the night she first heard the Mystery Singer talk. She met Sarah at the door with chatter about it. "I'm sure

82

I've heard that voice before. If I could just think where. I'll bet she's a movie star, or a radio star!" She stared at the radio as if it could reveal the secret.

A smile played around Sarah's lips as she watched her daughter's serious face. "What have you written for the singer's description?"

Helen wrinkled her brows. "I haven't sent my wrappers in yet; I've only got twenty."

"So I noticed; there's soap stacked all over the bathroom closet," Sarah laughed.

"Well, next week is the end of the contest, so I have to get a few more bars this week. But you know, Mother, I think she's a white person from the deep south."

Things changed for Sarah at the school. Dr. Bloom had operated on Jill's lip and done a beautiful job, for which all three were grateful. Then the doctor told Sarah, "We'd better get started on you, my dear. This week we'll use the electrolysis."

So Sarah's lessons were discontinued. It seemed incredible that so much could have happened to her in less than three months. She felt as changed as she looked; it was remarkable how happy one felt being able to do things, even simple everyday things like dancing and playing cards. And the knowledge of a slender figure—she had lost twenty-five pounds by now—and a good skin made a woman hold her head higher than she otherwise would, Sarah was very sure of that.

She walked with the grace of her model's training, and with the light step that came from vitality and happiness combined. "I suppose it's a matter of confidence—self-confidence," Sarah said to herself, and wanted to pinch herself to make sure it all wasn't a dream. If she felt like this now, how would she feel, she wondered, after the surgery was over and she actually had a pretty face?

She knew some qualms about that, just as she had known them over each new step she had taken. This was to be the most drastic; It was naturally frightening. Because for all the massages and molding and packs, bleaches, and facials, for all the exercise

83

and dieting and the changes they had wrought, the Sarah Davis she had lived with for so many years was still recognizable. What would that woman feel like in two weeks, when she looked into the mirror and saw someone she didn't know, somebody nobody else would recognize? What would Sarah Davis be like with a new hairline and thin brows set at an intriguing slant, a straight pretty nose, a lifted face?

She was to be ready for the final day of the Mystery Singer contest—the unveiling, far more literally than the studio manager or the Banner Soap people knew. She was to be ready to wear a new name, for the glamour-voiced Southern singer could not be called Sarah Davis. Instead Miss Julie Le Dere would be introduced to the audience of contestants, and whenever Sarah sang after that, she would be Julie Le Dere.

People would be calling her that; she would get mail under that name; it would be in the papers. So that was another thing Sarah Davis would have to get used to, and learn to carry off with aplomb.

Yes, she was sure to be shaking in her shoes more than one time before her new self became second nature.

Not once though, did Sarah think of backing out. She was too far in, and besides, that had never been her nature. She yearned to say something to Helen about this final step, to ask her daughter to love her just the same—but if she did, George might be told; Helen might worry; and then there'd be trouble. So she kept the last secret, and on the day that began her sessions with Dr. Bloom, Sarah, feeling a little like a spy with the handkerchief over his eyes and his back to the wall, gritted her teeth and accepted whatever was to come.

"Cinderella, here I come," she murmured. "Or should it be 'Here Comes Cinderella'?"

The doctor started with the operations that would be least noticeable to others, or would change Sarah less; hairline to be covered for a while yet by the old hairdo, removal of the blemishes; the little warts on her chin, electrolysis for the hair on her upper lip, plastic surgery on her ears; and they, too, hidden as yet. Sarah was amazed that so much could be done to her in such a short time, and that she felt very little pain from any of it. She watched for reactions from Helen and Dora.

"Mother, I do believe your little mustache is disappearing, and I like the way May plucked your eyebrows."

"Yo' mean the doc dehair you with all them needles astickin' in you, Miz Sarah?" That was after Sarah gave a lengthy account of the electrolysis. "Lordy, Lordy, you sure gone through lots o' misery for that man." Dora wagged her head in sympathy. "M-m-m, do y'all think Mistah Jawge is worth it?"

Sarah laughed softly. "You know, Dora, I did this all because of him; I thought if I was slim and pretty he would love me more. I was afraid I would lose him, but you know, now I don't care! Isn't that funny? Oh, I guess I love him, but believe me, Dora, the worm has turned."

Then came the lifting of the chin, bust and stomach. The nose would have to come last. Dr. Bloom brought her home Saturday evening, and she went to bed exhausted, excited and just the least bit conscious of the pain under the bandages on her breasts and stomach. She ran her hand lightly over the area and grinned to herself in the cover of darkness. "I'll be a little bit of Turner, Gable and Russell all rolled up in one!" She was not so frightened now; curiosity had the better of her. "I can't wait until my nose is fixed, and my hair." She dropped off to sleep with a vision of loveliness floating in front of her. The lady had silvery hair and she looked like an angel, beckoning Sarah to follow her, and yet, it seemed to Sarah that she was the angel.

The next morning, Helen discovered her Mother's double chin had disappeared, and she was as elated over her Mother's appearance as Sarah herself. "Gee Mummy, wait till Daddy sees how thin you are! And all the improvements on your face. Will he be surprised?" She hummed happily as she set the table. Her eyes travelled over the bulky wrapper Sarah had tied around her. "How much weight have you lost, Mother?"

Sarah caressed her new shape. "Oh, I'd say close to thirty

85

pounds. I didn't believe I could do it, but I did. I did the impossible."

Helen went to her and put her arms around the new slender figure. "I haven't got as much to hug, but I'm so glad for you."

The telephone rang as they were eating breakfast; Sarah's sister was calling from Iowa. "Can you come, Sarah? I'm just worn out taking care of Jerry and I thought you and Helen could spend a few weeks before Christmas. You could help me with Jerry and visit too." Helen's cousin Jerry had broken her leg and didn't really need nursing as much as she needed cheering up and companionship of her own age. "Please come, dear!"

Sarah bit her lip and held back the rush of words that she wanted to blurt out: "Oh, no, Mary, that would spoil every-thing."

Instead she said, "I know Helen will love to come, but I just can't Mary, not right away." And to herself she thought, "Honestly, things work out in the most peculiar way. This is a god-send!"

So it was arranged that Sarah would put Helen on the train and try to get to Des Moines later herself.

"Goodness, I'll have to call your father and tell him we're going to leave tomorrow morning." Sarah picked up the phone again.

Helen turned to her in astonishment. "You're going to tell Daddy *we're* going? But you just now told Aunt Mary you couldn't come!" She eyed her mother suspiciously.

"So I did, dear, and as far as your father is concerned, he must think I'm with you. I must stay here and finish my course, honey. I still have things to do." Helen would just have to accept that dictum without any explanation.

When he answered her call, George was very upset over Sarah's decision. "I'm coming home Friday night, dear! I hate to come home to an empty house."

Sarah smiled into the phone, "Well, why don't you get you a room at a hotel for a week or so. You can eat in cafés, see peo-

86

ple and you won't be so lonely." Things were going along in the right direction.

"H-m-mp, I hadn't thought about doing that. I probably will Sarah." George asked a few more questions, promised to call Sarah at her sister's home and then they said goodbye.

"Why Mother, how in the world can you talk to Daddy from Aunt Mary's house if you're down here?" Helen was puzzled.

"I won't dear. You will. Then you'll call me, and then I'll call him. Just tell him I'm out, shopping, visiting, or something. But please—keep my secret, until you come back," Sarah begged.

"I'll promise Mother, but you're getting more complicated by the minute." The girl went into her room and started to get her bags ready. "Jerry would have to have a broken leg when I visit her," she complained. Then she went to the door and called out, "Mother?"

Sarah went to her daughter's room. "Yes dear?" She sat down on the edge of the bed, where Helen was packing her bag.

"I'll miss a whole week of school. Our holiday vacation doesn't start until next week." She frowned as she folded up her lacy night gowns. "But I guess I can make it up."

"I'm sure you can, Helen, your record can take it. Whatever you do don't let on to your Daddy that I'm not there, and don't let Mary tell him anything. I'll write to her and explain everything."

"Don't worry Mother, I'll keep Daddy in the dark. May I have Ham over for dinner tonight, Mummy?" Her busy hands were still for a moment as she said sadly, "Gee, I won't get to see him for such a long time." Ham was the "One Man" in Helen's life, at the moment.

87

Chapter 12

THE TRAIN FOR IOWA LEFT UNION STATION AT SIX A.M. SARAH AND
Helen took a cab from the house. Sarah had last minute instructions for her daughter. As Helen was going up the steps, Sarah
called out, "Be careful dear, don't talk to any strangers. I'll call
you soon." Sarah stood beside the moving train, weeping a few
tears. It was the first time she and Helen had ever been separated.
She was still a baby, to Sarah's thinking.

Back home Sarah prepared her own breakfast, waiting for
Dora. Her mind busy making plans. She would stay until Friday
morning, send a few of her things to a hotel, give Dora a paid
vacation, and then—she grinned to herself—and then, "Enter
Miss Julie Le Dere." Her eyes held a wicked glint.

One thing worried her; how was she going to have her nose
fixed and her cheeks lifted, and sing on the same day. Doctor
Bloom suggested, "Come back after your appointment tonight
Mrs. Davis, I'll operate and by tomorrow evening you'll be able
to carry on. What is so important that you can't be excused one
evening?" he asked.

But Sarah kept her secret, and she sang the next day, heavily
veiled, and in pain. Every time she opened her mouth, it hurt,
but no one knew, not even Fellows. The next day her face didn't
bother her. She kept to herself as she looked like a fugitive from
an accident.

She spent hours talking with Mr. Domere about her education she had just finished. He was very pleased the way she had grasped everything he had offered. "Truthfully, Mrs. Davis, I had my doubts if you'd stick it out, but you surprised me. You've made so many friends and so many opportunities will come your way now."

Sarah laughed softly, "Please Mr. Domere, I've already started that 'merry chase,' you predicted." Domere looked at her bandaged face curiously, Sarah went on, "It's almost over, so I guess I can tell you a secret. Have you heard the Mystery Singer?" He shook his head no. "Well you listen today at four on station W.L.S. I'm the Mystery Singer. Fellows arranged it. I've got to be ready for the unveiling this coming week. The contest closes Monday night. I hope I'll be ready." She had so much to do yet.

"Well I'll be darned, so you've already got a job on the radio." He slapped his knee and gazed at her soft blue eyes with frank admiration. "And remember Mrs. Davis you did this with your 'old' face."

They both laughed over his remark. Sarah had brought it up so many times in the past. She took some envelopes out of her bag, "Here is some of my fan mail as 'Mystery Lady.' I received one from my daughter yesterday, and it did my heart a world of good." She passed them on to Domere. He read them, smiling at the compliments Sarah had received.

"Do you mean your own daughter doesn't know this 'Lovely Lady' is you?" Domere had never met such a woman before. She could keep secrets.

"No, 'course I would have liked for her to know, but it wouldn't have been fair. And I also have an offer from a night club to sing as their specialty singer." Sarah giggled like a school girl.

Dora was curious to see Miz Sarah's nose, but the bandages wouldn't come off until the end of the week, so she would have to wait until she came back from her vacation. Thursday night Sarah bid her maid goodbye, "Here's your salary for three weeks, Dora, and you deserved it, dear. Without you I'd never have made the radio. I'll have a nice surprise for you Christmas eve, but I'll call you and tell you when to come back."

Friday morning Sarah packed a few things into two bags; her cosmetics, and a few clothes. She locked up the old gray car in the garage, called a cab and locked up the house. "Take me to the Stevens Hotel, driver."

The desk clerk looked curiously at Sarah's heavily veiled face. The bell hop lifted the bags Sarah indicated. It all looked rather suspicious, but Sarah didn't offer any explanation. Installed in her pleasant, but definitely not choice room, she unpacked her bags, and left for school.

Dr. Bloom removed the bandages and Sarah was delirious with joy. Even with her mousey brown hair, bangs and all, she looked like a pretty stranger. "Gee, I'm not sure it's me." She felt her face carefully, gropingly, "It's all right, healed and everything?" She appealed to Doctor Bloom like a little kid, a scared little kid. This was too much like hocus pocus.

Dr. Bloom assured her that all was well. "I did a fancy job, if I do say so myself; no scars, no redness, and lifting your face and removing your blemishes, makes you look like a young lady, a very beautiful young lady." He smiled at her reflection in the mirror. "You would never believe you were the same woman that came in here three months ago."

"I wonder if my husband will be able to recognize me?" Sarah was still worried. "Do you think he could?"

"He'd have to be a mind reader if he did. You'll just have to remember to act differently, talk differently, and think differently," he cautioned her.

"Like this," then Sarah lit a cigarette, blew a cloud of smoke at the ceiling and drawled with her southern accent, "Come up and see me sometime."

The doctor laughed, "I see you have the right idea and I do like your southern accent. Just wait until May gets your hair fixed," he promised.

May gave Sarah a permanent first, then bleached and dyed her hair. The skin around the hair line, where Dr. Bloom had made the tiny incisions, became red and inflamed. May was worried and Sarah was frantic, "What if I get an infection, what if it makes a scar?"

But the doctor waved away all their troubles by treating the faint lines with some soothing liquid. "Wash your face for the next few days with witch hazel. Apply this ointment. By Monday morning you'll feel like this face has always been yours."

May had cut Sarah's hair very short, gave her a tight cold wave. After the pin curls had dried and May was removing the bobby pins, Sarah looked at the girl in the mirror and two big tears rolled down the fresh young cheeks. "I hope I haven't done wrong. What if Helen doesn't like me. Maybe George will leave me now." She cried into the kleenex May offered her.

"Oh, come on now, lady, you've been such a good sport all this while, don't get the winwams now. It couldn't be undone. So you just better start smiling and admiring yourself. You're going to look like a movie star when you get made-up, false eyelashes, and some high class clothes." May curled the little silvery ringlets over her finger, then she took her rat tailed comb and ran it through Sarah's pretty hair deliberately mussing it up. "There now it looks just like natural curly hair. My aren't you something to stare at." May stood back and admired her handiwork and Sarah's flustered and confused face.

She watched Sarah's soft white manicured hand, reach up and touch the lovely curls that covered her queenly head. The pretty pink ears, were small and lay close to the head. The small heart shaped face was young, and appealing. The skin was clear and fresh as a child's. May had combed a slight fringe of curly bangs over the widow's peak. It gave Sarah's face a saucy touch. Sarah looked closely at her mouth, and remarked, "Even my mouth looks different."

"Well, it's bound to. Dr. Bloom had to lift your cheeks and naturally it gives your mouth a different expression. Just like your eyebrows have sort of an oriental slant. Your eyes tilt at the corners slightly, but they are the only feature that you can say you started out with." May squinted her eyes at Sarah, thinking,

91

then advised, "If I were you I'd wear false eyelashes all the time, because you have such soft mild blue eyes, they might be recognized. Lashes will widen and deepen the eyes." She wrote something down on her pad. "I'll order you a couple of strips and show you how to put them on. Do you want me to make you up Monday?"

"Oh yes, and Tuesday, too. I have a special date Tuesday. That will be the official unveiling of my new self." In more ways than one, Sarah thought.

She left the school after May had finished her hair and went to an exclusive dress shop. She sat in a luxurious lounge and watched mannikins parade up and down in front of her. Sarah chose a sport outfit, a suit, an evening gown and a dress she could wear any time. She chose the proper accessories, with the help of the saleslady. She tried the clothes on and walked about as she had been taught. Even the saleslady was impressed, "You must be traveling incognito; no make-up, heavy black veil." She looked at Sarah for an explanation.

"Yes I am, I've just had an operation on my nose and can't wear make-up as yet."

"Are you a movie star, or a model?" The woman was curious. Sarah was so beautiful, and yet her clothes were so out of line with her looks.

"Yes in a way. I'm a singer." Sarah glowed all over with pride. Even the sales people noticed she was something special.

"Oh how thrilling. Where do you sing?" She was all ears.

"Over the radio, W.L.S." Sarah completed her shopping, undergarments, nightgowns, house coats, negligees, hose, everything she thought she would need until she could shop around. Of course the saleswoman showed her the best, the latest and the most beautiful. Sarah gave her a check and told her to send it to the Stevens Hotel, room one hundred and two. Sarah hoped she had chosen wisely. She had never had time or money to indulge in feathers, chiffons, silks, satins and lacy things, before, but now she had to choose for Miss Julie Le Dere. "I've got to

92

remember that I'm not just plain, old homely Sarah Davis anymore. I'm a personage, I've got a reputation to live up to."

She went back to the hotel and waited for the shop to send her new clothes over, then called in a maid and had her press her new suit. She rolled up all her old things and handed them to the girl saying, "Please give these to someone in need, or else throw them out." As the girl departed with the bundle, Sarah said softly, "Goodbye Sarah Davis." She danced to the mirror and bowed to the beautiful creature looking back at her. She hugged herself and began humming, "I get ideas, I get ideas, M-m-m-m," and she tangoed around the room.

Helen called her as she was dressing, "Mother, how are you? I haven't heard from you, since the day I got here. One phone call, I thought you were going to write to me, and call me."

It was obvious that her daughter was in a huff. "Oh darling, I've been so busy and rather incapacitated at times. I had my nose operated on and I couldn't do much."

Helen's excited voice came over the stretch of wires, "Oh Mother, how do you look?"

"Everyone assures me I'm quite a doll. I've bought some new, very swank clothes, and I have my hair done differently. Oh, I've got a big surprise for you, chicken, Wait until you see your old Mother." Sarah's face beamed as she heard Helen's merry giggle.

"Oh Mother, before I forget, Daddy called. He's staying at the Lawrence Hotel, and he was kind of huffy, when you weren't here. He's called twice." They talked a few minutes more, Helen asking about Ham, and the Mystery Lady, Sarah about her sister and niece.

Then Sarah told Helen, "I'll call your Daddy, I want him to think the call came from Des Moines. Then, listen dear, I'm going to get me a room at the Lawrence, too. But remember, I don't want your Daddy to find out." Then she remembered, "Ask for Miss Le Dere when you call."

Helen giggled, "What are you going to do Mummy, get the goods on him? Why don't you just hire a detective. It'd be easier," she suggested. "And why the *nom de guerre?*" Helen studied French.

Sarah immediately called the Lawrence Hotel. George's voice was gruff as he answered Sarah's pleasant, "Hello dear."

He started out finding fault just like he always did.

"Sarah I have called you twice this morning. Where were you? I suppose Helen does all the work and you and Mary just gad about." And so it went, Sarah just smiled smugly and let him rave. She told him she'd call him, from now on.

"I hope there won't be too much of that from now on. The food in the restaurant is terrible. Besides we've got a perfectly nice home sitting out there alone," he griped.

After her conversation with George, Sarah called the Lawrence Hotel back. "I'd like to reserve an apartment or a suite if you have one available for Monday, late?"

They promised her a small apartment; bedroom, sitting room, and tiny kitchen. Sarah was delighted. "Now I can do my own cooking, and be close to George. Who knows what will happen?"

She dressed in her new suit, still wore a veil, but over an adorable new velvet hat. Sarah had to go up to Fellows and announce her presence.

"Now don't look so startled, Mr. Fellows, you knew this was coming." She dropped her eyes as his keen glance swept over her figure, her clothes and the beau-catching ringlets peeping beneath the smart little calot.

He drew a long whistle. "Wow, I had no-o-o idea, what you would look like after your transformation." He stood back and looked some more. "M-m-m, maybe they could do something for me too."

Fellows took her elbow and guided her into the elevator. Sarah shivered from the slight pressure of his big hand. "I wonder how I'll affect George," she thought.

In the room where she broadcasted from, Sarah removed her small hat and ran her fingers through the silvery curls. Fellows stood there watching her. It was unbelievable that this was the woman he had first brought up there; fat, homely, dowdy and

94

ordinary. Now, she was like a delicate flower, lovely, ethereal and out of this world. She really had turned out to be a mystery lady. No one would have described her as she was before anyway. Now her face and figure went with her sweet, haunting voice. Before and after; Fellows thought about the comparison, and swallowed his laugh. Sarah was on the air. "Why I could get this delicious looking morsel all the singing dates she could handle."

Sarah was tired and nervous after her radio engagement. Fellows wanted her to go someplace where they could talk, but Sarah insisted she go straight to the Hotel. "I'm so tired Mr. Fellows. Remember I've been going through the mill for the last two weeks, and I'm at the end of my rope." She stepped out of the cab, at the entrance of the swank Hotel, saying to the disgruntled young man, standing beside her, "I'll talk to you Monday, remember, we have a big date. It's the end of the contest. I'll be at the school about three o'clock."

"What are you going to do this week-end?" he asked, hat in hand.

Sarah giggled behind her veil, "He's fishing for a date, of all things." To him she said, "I'm going to get me some magazines and relax. I might sleep from now until Monday morning." Then she was gone.

But Sarah had too much to do, to waste Saturday by sleeping. She was up early. First she went shopping, perfumes, more clothes, a long jeweled cigarette holder, and a lot of luxuries she had never had before. Then she went to an agency and hired a colored maid. Her name was Velvet. She was a professional ladies' maid, being able to dress hair, apply make-up and cook. Then Sarah went into a detective agency and talked to the man in charge. She told him her story and gave him proof of the authenticity of what she told him. "I want a man that can act as my escort, as a detective, and maybe, in some other category." She smiled at the man sitting across from her, as he said:

"I'd apply for the job myself, dear lady, but what you want I guess is some handsome young fellow."

95

"No, not too young, about thirty-five or so. Just so he's handsome."

Maybe she'd have to make George jealous. "I'll be at the Lawrence Hotel Monday until two. You can send someone over for me to interview. Just have him ask for Miss Le Dere." She swept out of the office, leaving the man behind the desk wishing he could recapture his youth.

Sarah enjoyed a leisurely dinner in a quiet café and then with a best seller under her arm, walked back to the hotel. She took a warm bath, carefully cleaned her face as the doctor had advised, and put on one of her new gowns and negligees and curled up on the bed. She opened the book and then laid it down and reached for the telephone.

"Give me long distance please," she asked the switchboard operator. In a few minutes Helen's sweet voice reached her mother's ears.

"Oh Mummy, I'm so glad you called. I've been homesick all day."

Sarah could detect tears in her precious child's voice. "Now Helen is that any way for you to act. What's the matter? Are you sick?" That was the first thing Sarah always thought of, when Helen felt bad.

"No, just homesick. I heard from Ham, and he's going to a football rally tonight. I'll bet he'll dance with some of those old goonies that I don't like."

Sarah smiled. So that was it, Helen was jealous. "Darling, can't you and Jerry invite some friends in and make fudge or something?"

When she hung up, Helen was in better spirits, especially as Sarah promised to send her and Jerry a surprise package Monday.

Then, just for curiosity's sake, Sarah called the Lawrence Hotel. "Mr. Davis? Just a minute I'll see if he's in." The clerk rang several times, then George answered, "I have a call for you sir."

Sarah butted in then real quick, so George would think it was an out-of-town connection. "George—Sarah. The clerk rang several times, dear, I thought you were out of the hotel." Sarah bit her lips to keep the laughter back.

"H-m-m-p, no dear, I was in the bathroom shaving. I thought I might go to a show, nothing to do around here," he complained.

"Oh you'll meet someone that you can play cards with, or while a few hours away with. There are so many nice people you can meet," she suggested, with her tongue in her cheek.

"Oh I suppose so. What is Helen doing?" he inquired.

"She and Jerry have some friends in. They are playing games and making fudge," she hoped.

"Well, tell her I love her and I'll be glad when you come home. By the way how long do you intend to stay up there?" He sounded like a spoiled little boy.

"We just got here George. Maybe we'll come home in a week or so. I'll call you in a couple of days. We'll see dear. Good night." Sarah hung up, convulsed with laughter.

The book was interesting, but Sarah's eyes kept closing. She took off her frilly negligee, then crawled into the clean comfortable bed. "M-m-m, this is the life," she murmured sleepily as the telephone shrilled through the stillness. "Oh good grief, who can that be." She jumped out of bed and grabbed the phone.

"Miss Le Dere?"

"Huh, oh yes, this is she." For a minute she forgot who she was.

"Jim Fellows," came the deep masculine voice. "I asked for Mrs. Davis first, and the clerk had no one registered under that name, so I thought you might be using your Mystery Lady's name. I called up to see if you'd like to go dancing with me."

"Tonight?" Sarah looked down at her night gown. "Oh I'd love to but I'm already tucked in for the night. Maybe next week, Jim."

He couldn't change her mind so he finally hung up. Sarah went back to bed, and laughed gleefully, "And to think, it's just beginning!"

97

Chapter 13

MONDAY MORNING SHE CHECKED OUT OF THE HOTEL AND TOOK A
cab to the Lawrence. She still wore the veil: suppose she ran
into George. He might recognize her. But then how could he,
when she didn't see anything in the mirror that resembled the
old Sarah Davis? She was muddled up, for nothing had quite
changed inside her, yet.

The clerk looked at the smartly dressed lady with the black
veil. "Yes Ma'am, I have a suite reserved for Miss Le Dere. I
have already sent your maid up to your apartment, Madam." He
motioned to a bell hop to take Sarah's bags. She had them filled
to the top this time. The clerk watched Sarah's trim ankles as she
walked to the elevator. "My oh my, I'll bet she's straight from
Hollywood."

Sarah tipped the boy, and then turned around to greet Velvet.
"I hope you'll like our temporary home Velvet." Sarah talked
with her sweet southern accent.

"Yes, Madam, it is a lovely apartment. So convenient, and
roomy." She showed Sarah through the rooms. In one corner of
the dressing room, was a cot for Velvet. The kitchen was small,
but so compact. "Yes'm, we'll get along splendidly." Velvet spoke
beautiful English, so different from Dora, who was a colored
woman born in the slums of Georgia, and had "jest growed up."
It was very evident that Velvet had tasted the better things in life.

98

"Now Velvet, I want you to address me as Miss Julie; you have been with me a long time, just in case anyone inquires. Also, I am a model, and a singer." Sarah took off her hat and eased her small, perfect shape into a big chair. She crossed a silken leg and opened her bag. Out came the long jeweled cigarette holder and carefully she placed a king size cigarette in it. Then she took her tiny lighter and lit it. She blew rings at the ceiling awhile before she turned to watch Velvet. "M-m-m, I suppose I've crushed everything, I'll have to get more luggage."

"Now don't you worry your pretty head, Miss Julie, I'll restore these garments in no time." She was a good-looking woman, large but well shaped. She was wearing a gray uniform with dainty lace cuffs, collar and apron. "Where have we been Miss Julie and where are we going, just in case?" She looked over a pile of fluffy feathers.

Sarah laughed, "M-m-m, yes we've got to have a past and a future, don't we?" She smoked slowly, meditating, then she answered Velvet. "We've just come from New York. Before that we were in Hollywood, where I sang in some famous night spot." She puffed some more. "Right at the present we are going to stay here, as I have some modeling engagements." This double life she was leading, was getting more confusing as the days went by. From now on, she was Julie Le Dere, she mustn't forget her southern accent. There were so many things she had to remember.

She went to the phone and asked for the number she had looked up in the telephone directory. While she waited Velvet went about her work, but Sarah knew she was listening. She asked the voice, "I would like to find out about the method of renting your gowns and jewelry." Sarah ended the conversation by saying, "I'll be there at 4:30. Thank you."

To Velvet she explained, "I intend to entertain a lot, go out, and of course sing. I'll need a lot more evening gowns than I have, so I decided to rent some." She danced around the room, happy beyond words. She stopped at the mirror and admired the smiling stranger. It was hard for her to realize that it was really she.

Velvet asked, "Miss Julie excuse me for asking, but do you ever use make-up?"

"Yes, Velvet, in fact I intend to be made-up today. I've had a nose operation, so I haven't touched my face more than necessary."

"Oh yes'm, well whenever you're ready, I'll be glad to help you."

Sarah was too restless and filled with anticipation to sit still. She was forever wandering to the mirror. She fussed with her curls, pursed up her mouth, sang part of a song. If she looked this beautiful without make-up how would she look with it. She was happy, for the first time in her life, about her own personal self.

She had Velvet order lunch sent up from the kitchen, saying, "Tomorrow I'll have you go shopping for a few snacks."

Right after lunch, the man came from the detective agency. He was tall, dark and handsome. Sarah couldn't have picked an escort any better. She smiled at him as she noticed his manicured nails, his sharp blue eyes, tailor made suit, and winning smile. Ah, yes he'd do. "I'd like to have you take me some place for dinner, to start off with. There's someone staying in this hotel that I want you to keep an eye on, and it might be better if you took a room here."

The fellow's name was Tom Masters. He asked in a pleasantly gruff voice, "Shall I call you by your first name?"

"Yes you might as well call me Julie, and I'll call you Tom. Later you will probably be my manager or agent or someone that looks after me. I'll tell you all about it over dinner tonight."

At three o'clock Sarah slipped into the Salon without anyone seeing her. May was ready and waiting. "M-m-m, one of these days we'll dye your lashes. Your eyebrows are real black but your lashes are a little lighter. We'll put mascara on them today." She cleaned Sarah's skin thoroughly, then she applied a light foundation base, rouge, delicately tinted powder, lipstick and then the false eyelashes. Then she lightly touched the brows with the mascara brush, and then went over the lashes. Next she combed Sarah's silver curls and stood back to admire the effect. "Gee whiz, wait till Domere sees you. He's been asking all day if you came in." She laughed as she began putting her boxes and bottles away. "You haven't seen anyone since you had your bandages off have you?"

Sarah was sitting there looking in the mirror at the dazzling creature reflected therein. May walked back to the vanity, "Hey wake up, it's you." She waved her hand in front of Sarah's eyes.

"I thought I saw a ghost for a minute. Don't you think I resemble Jean Harlow?" May came back and studied Sarah's glamorous face again.

Her voice held a note of awe as she said, "My God, you do. It's been so long since I've seen any pictures of her, it never dawned on me." She watched Sarah get up and walk to the mirror across the room. "You have Jean Harlow's face, Jane Russell's bosom, Betty Grable's hips and Lana Turner's legs. That adds up to Julie Le Dere. That's a cute name. I'll bet you before long it'll be in all the papers." She fussed around Sarah's curls, "With a face and a shape like you got, you'll be somebody important."

Sarah walked down the long hall to the reception room, Thack was leaning over a book, reading. Sarah coughed a little and waited for the gray haired woman to look up. "Pardon me, but can you tell me where I might find Mr. Domere?" The southern sweetness was poured on thick.

Thack dropped her book, stood up and remembering her manners, asked politely, "Won't you be seated. I'll find him." She looked Sarah over again and backed out of the room. It took all Sarah had to keep from bursting out in a tell-tale laugh. Thack had no idea who she was.

She came back presently with Domere in tow. She had told him excitedly, "I'll swear if I didn't know Jean Harlow was dead, I'd say she was out in my office right now."

When Domere approached Sarah in a very courteous manner,

Sarah had to pinch herself, to keep her face straight. "Mr. Domere?"

"Yes, may I have the privilege to be of service." He hadn't talked that way, when he had first met her.

"This is a modeling agency I believe?" He nodded. "I have just arrived from Hollywood and I thought you might be able to place me."

"Oh yes of course, I'm sure for one so charming, we will be able and delighted to, of course. Just a minute until I call my assistant." He went to Thack's desk and pushed a buzzer. Miss Baer came right out. Domere turned to his assistant and asked, "Miss Baer this young lady is a model, just arrived from Hollywood. Do you think we could find a suitable engagement for her?"

Miss Baer looked Sarah over, and said enthusiastically, "I should say so, Mr. Domere. We have several exclusive fashion salons looking for just her type."

"Shall we go into my office Miss—" Domere hesitated.

Sarah started to laugh and announced, "I'm Julie Le Dere."

Domere knew her proposed name, and when he finally realized it was Sarah Davis standing there, he nearly fainted. The women, too, were dumbfounded. Sarah laughed until she had to sit down. "Well, say something. Do you like the results of our experiment?"

If Sarah had any doubts about her beauty and her new face, they all vanished when she heard the exclamations and compliments from the three in front of her. Domere grinned and rubbed his hands, "Have you ever seen anything so utterly gorgeous in this office before?" he demanded.

Thack had her arm around Sarah, telling her how wonderful it was that her dream had come true, just like she had planned it. "It's uncanny, Sarah, simply uncanny."

Miss Baer held her hand out to Sarah, "You deserve every bit of praise and glory lady, you really earned it. Now get up and strut your stuff, if you really want that job."

Sarah looked at her with her mouth slightly ajar, "You mean you thought I was serious about that job?"

"Well, maybe you were fooling, but I wasn't. Do you want to model beautiful clothes, pose for famous photographers, and have your glamorous puss on every magazine in the nation? Come on now, show me how you look in your role."

Sarah walked across the room in her most dramatic performance. "Splendid. You can make them all sit up and take notice. Let's go in and talk business now." Miss Baer was more than anxious.

Sarah laughed gaily, and jumped to her feet, "Thank you so much, Miss Baer. I'll have to take a rain check on that job. Right now I've got to go to the radio studio."

Her eyes found Mr. Domere's. "Tonight the contest closes, so I'll reveal a big secret. I'm the Mystery Lady and I have to be at the studio, to sing my southern songs."

Thack bubbled over with goodwill for her future, "Oh I hope you keep on singing lady, I just love to listen to you. And I love your southern accent. It sounds so romantic."

They laughed at the austere woman going lovey-dovey on them. Miss Baer was delighted that Sarah was not only a perfect model, but a charming singer as well. "Do you have any more talents tucked up your sleeves, my dear lady?"

Domere put his arm around Sarah's shapely shoulders.

"And I thought you probably wrote your speech from some article in a book," Miss Baer admitted. "You're not only beautiful but brainy too. And that reminds me, Paul, just because Sarah is such a lovely young lady, you don't have to take advantage of it."

Sarah smiled; where had she heard those words before? She remembered that she had wondered if she would ever enjoy an experience like that. Funny how things work out. If you want something bad enough, it will happen.

Fellows came in looking for her, and she had to run, but not before she told Miss Baer she'd drop in and see her in the morning.

"Don't look so flabbergasted, Jim, it's still me, with a little make-up on." He frightened her with the heartsick look in his eyes.

"You're so beautiful, Julie, I thought about you all night. Give me the chance to see you, to be with you." He grabbed her arm as they entered the lobby of the radio building.

They stopped, Sarah trying to break his hold, "Please Jim, I'm still the little homely woman you first met as Sarah Davis, remember?"

"I never heard of her. First I fell in love with your voice, now with your lovely face, your beautiful body." His eyes devoured her.

"Oh please, stop talking like that, I feel naked—I've got to go, I'll be late." She broke from him and ran for the elevator. He followed.

In the broadcasting room, he never took his eyes off her face. For the first time, she was nervous and ill at ease. She laughed a little as she spoke over the air. Sadly, slowly, she addressed the unseen thousands, perhaps millions, listening to her, "Dear friends, as you know this is goodbye for a while. I've enjoyed playing for you, singing songs about my dear southland, talking to you for a moment. I've enjoyed it more than you'll ever know, and I hope I've brought you a little happiness, so I'll close by saying I wish you could all win this wonderful contest we've been in, and now I'll say good night and God bless you. Tomorrow night you will see me, the Mystery Lady in person."

Fellows took her arm and led her out. Sarah was crying—partly because she was so happy and yet so afraid of the dangers that lay in her path.

Fellows insisted on going into the Hotel lobby with her, but Sarah would have none of him, "Go home please Jim, and let me be. I'm too upset to talk to you, about anything." She glanced around the lobby. Perhaps George would be down there. Her eyes traveled over the men sitting there, lonely, passing the hours until bedtime, some of them smoking, some reading, a few watching the others. Sarah noticed quite a few masculine eyes turn in her direction. And then, the door opened and George Davis came in. Sarah held her breath and stared at him, he passed close enough for her to touch him.

Fellows was holding her arm and talking passionately, tenderly in her ear. "Please let me come up for a few minutes, Julie, you don't know anything about me. Give me a chance."

But Sarah wasn't listening, her eyes were following the figure of her arrogant husband. George stopped at the desk, got his key and walked to the elevator. Sarah turned swiftly and hurried after him. Jim Fellows stood there, crestfallen and stymied.

The desk clerk scraped and bowed as Sarah swept by. Velvet had been doing a little talking, evidently.

Sarah reached the elevator just as the doors slid open. George stepped back as Sarah approached. The elevator boy grinned as he said, "Good evening Miss Le Dere." His eyes showed his admiration.

"M-m-m, my fame sweeps before me like a burning flame." She grinned back at him. George had removed his hat and was observing her out of the corner of his eye. Sarah laughed down inside. He looked so pompous, so sort of married looking. Maybe she was prejudiced, being his wife for so long. She held her gloved hand to her lips, she wanted to laugh so badly she could have died. George called his floor and the boy stopped so quickly it caught Sarah off balance and she bumped into George's stocky body. He reached out his hand to steady her. Sarah murmured in her southern voice, "Oh I'm sorry, I didn't mean to knock you over." She fluttered her long lashes at him.

She could see the deep red flush creep up his neck. She'd have to warn him about high blood pressure. George smiled at the lovely dream clinging to his arm. His eyes weren't too sure they could focus, but he'd try. He gulped and managed to gasp, "Delighted to help you." He bowed himself out the door.

Again Sarah's gloved hand stole to her mouth as the boy turned and winked at her, "You nearly slayed him, Miss Le Dere."

It took Sarah half the night to recover from George's reaction to her pretty face. If he could have known the truth, but of course he didn't. He would never dream that Sarah and the girl he held in the elevator, were one and the same. She sighed happily, she had passed the test with flying colors.

The next morning, Sarah slept late and when she awakened, Velvet had her bath ready, her breakfast ordered and even helped her dress. She combed her hair, and put her make-up on. "Gee Velvet you'll spoil me."

"I want to Miss Julie, I've waited on a lot of those Hollywood glamour girls, but they couldn't hold a candle to you."

"Velvet—did you just happen to give out a little information at the desk yesterday?" Sarah inquired laughingly. "I felt like the Queen of England, the way the clerk and the elevator boy salaamed in front of me." She peeked up at Velvet, who was busily curling each little silver ringlet, so carefully.

She answered meekly, "Yes'm I guess I did throw them a little bone to chew on. Someone has to ring a bell for you, Miss Julie."

Miss Julie let a little moan escape, "I'm afraid it's going to turn into a fire alarm before it's all over."

She was so upset the night before, that she had forgotten completely about her appointment with the Costume Shop. She would have forgotten about her dinner engagement if Velvet hadn't taken over. They had dined in the Pump Room, danced and spent a pleasant evening, but in one way it had been wasted. George probably had gone to bed right after his dinner. No she was using the wrong technique. She called Tom Master's room, "I want you to shadow the gentleman in room ten-twenty. His name is George Davis. I want to know where he goes, does, and so on."

"Velvet, please bring me my coat I'm going out, but I'll be back before I go to the radio studio."

She caught a cab at the entrance, the doorman handed her in as though she were Jean Harlow in person. "This is all right," she waved her eyelashes at him.

At the costume shop, Sarah chose gowns, jewels, furs and all the extra costumes she felt she would need, but couldn't afford to buy. The rental was very high, but the clothes were beautifully made. Some of the gowns, the manager informed her, came from the latest pictures. "These gowns have been worn by the most famous stars."

The jewelry looked so real to Sarah, she could hardly believe they were just copies of famous originals. She had locked her two modest rings in the lock box the last time she had visited the bank. She chose diamonds for the left hand, and emeralds and diamonds for the right, then bracelets, necklaces, earrings and hair ornaments.

The furs took Sarah's eyes, she tried on minks, finally choosing a silvery blue mink that just set her hair off like a neon light. Then a black flared short coat for day wear, stand up collar, huge cuffs, so chic on her tiny figure. It was made out of silky broadtail. Next came an evening wrap. Sarah chose a white ermine, so beautiful that she held her breath, as she slowly turned in front of the big mirror. "Oh, a Queen must have owned this." Her hands caressed the rich fur.

"You mean some Queen wishes she could own it," the manager corrected her. "Not too many women have them."

Sarah groaned inwardly as she looked at her bank account. She would have to accomplish her motive as quickly as possible.

"I'll have these things delivered immediately," he promised her.

Next Sarah stopped at the Salon. Thack was alone in the reception room. "My dear, I'm so glad to see you. Do you know you are the ten day wonder around here. Grayson was disappointed that he missed you. Why don't you play the same joke on him."

Sarah smiled, "Gee that sounds like fun. Does he have an appointment soon?"

Thack and Sarah bent over the appointment sheet. "Yes in ten minutes he is supposed to give a lesson to a Miss Loretta Hapgood. Suppose you go in and tell him that you are Miss Hapgood. He won't know the difference, because I took this over the phone." Thack gave her a little push towards the hall.

Sarah crossed her fingers and held them up for Thack to see.

At the door she knocked and Bob Grayson opened the door and looked at Sarah, a vision of loveliness. His warm brown eyes lit up with admiration as he gazed at her. "I'm Miss Hapgood, I have an appointment with you."

He waved her in, and answered softly, "Ah, yes indeed."

Grayson went to the phonograph and then asked, "What do you want to learn?"

"Well, first let's try a tango, do you have 'I Get Ideas'?"

Soon the tantalizing strains filled the room, Bob Grayson held out his arms, and Sarah went into them. They danced like one, it was heaven, and then the music ended. Bob Grayson laughed, "Do you know I could swear I've danced with you before. It's uncanny." His eyes swept over her beautiful body, and then back to her face. "But it can't be, because if I had ever held anyone as lovely as you are, I'd remember it the rest of my days."

That speech warmed the cockles of Sarah's heart. Then they did the bolero—then a waltz—then a fox-trot—the samba, the rumba, and so on until, Sarah decided the real Miss Hapgood would barge in any minute. "Well, what's wrong with my dancing. What do I need?" She fluttered her long black lashes demurely at Grayson.

He looked down at the haunting heart shaped face and vowed, "You're perfect, you're out of this world."

Sarah laughed in a low throaty way and pulled her hand loose from his. "Thank you, Mr. Grayson, you've been a wonderful teacher."

His eyes devoured her, "A teacher—then you, no it can't be, it isn't possible——" he stuttered helplessly.

Sarah came to his rescue, "You mean you don't believe it was possible to turn an ugly caterpillar into a pretty butterfly. It isn't impossible, it just took longer." Then she went to him and put her hand in his. "Yes, I am Sarah Davis, or really I am Julie Le Dere now."

"But the way you talk." He still couldn't believe her.

"I'm really from the deep south, so it wasn't hard for me to recapture my accent."

"It's intriguing, but then the whole 'You' is bewitching. Oh where can I see you again. We simply must go dancing." His eyes begged her, his hands held hers possessively.

"I'm staying at the Lawrence, Bob," and then she was gone.

Sarah laughed to herself all the way back to the hotel. "At least he always pretended he liked me even when I was homely, but then, he's a real gentleman."

When she entered the lobby she looked around for George, but he was nowhere in sight. Sarah sighed, time was running out and she had to do something quick. Maybe Tom would have some ideas.

Velvet had several messages to deliver. "A Mr. Fellows called, you are to call him back, so soon as you come in. Then a Mr. Masters called, he left a number." Velvet had it all written down on the pad. "These flowers came from a man by the name of George Davis." She indicated a vase filled with beautiful red roses.

Sarah threw her coat on a chair and hurried over to the table where the flowers were, "Oh no, this is too good to be true. Was there a card Velvet?" She read the card the maid handed her. It read "I hope we bump into each other again." "Why the old fox," Sarah fumed to herself, "I wonder if he uses that method on all the pretty girls he meets." She took a deep whiff of the roses, "At least he knows how to pick them." She wasn't sure if she meant the roses, or the girls.

"This box of candy came from Mr. Fellows." Velvet grinned from ear to ear, "And it isn't even Christmas yet."

"Order lunch, Velvet, and leave about a hundred calories off, I want to taste this candy." She tore the wrapping off and drooled over the big fat pieces of chocolate, the most delicious, the most delectable candy made, and also the most fattening, and the most tempting. She finally selected one and ate it slowly and relished every second of it. "Jim Fellows knows I'm on a diet, he's just tempting me, the meany." She ran her hand over her stomach. "Dr. Bloom warned me, there wouldn't be a two way stretch any more."

Sarah sat down by the phone and looked at her flowers and the five pound box of candy, "That's the first time I ever received gifts, for nothing." It was sort of nice to be beautiful.

Fellows talked long and ardently. After the unveiling he wanted to take her to some cozy spot so they could talk business. He had an offer for her—two hundred a week. "Well if you're sure it's business Jim, I'll go. But please don't make love to me any more. I'm not your type and besides I'm too old for you."

Velvet listening, looked at Sarah like she had lost her mind, "Why she could be any man's type, and what is she talking to, a man or a baby—too old for him." She laughed softly as she hung up the coat Sarah had worn. Then she set the table in the cozy living room.

Sarah jumped up and exclaimed, "You know Velvet, I've just got to have a piano. I wonder if they have one in the hotel I can use." She went back to the phone and called the manager.

"Why yes, we have a small grand we could let you use."

Then she called Tom Masters, "I don't know why you're interested in that old duffer, all he does is hang around a pool hall and read papers. Right now he's in his room sleeping." Tom was disgusted.

Sarah sighed as she hung up. How was she going to drag George out where she could get a hold on him. Then a brilliant idea came to her. "Velvet I want you to go out and get a fryer and about five o'clock, have it all ready and take it to Mr. Davis in room ten-twenty with my compliments. I'll show you just how I want it prepared."

"Miss Julie, excuse me for asking, but is Mr. Davis the gentlemen we are aiming to please?" Her black face was wreathed in a big smile.

"Yes Velvet, he's the victim. Don't ever tell him too much, but be as nice and sweet as you can be to him. Remember he's the King bee." Sarah laughed mischievously.

"He must have lots of money, Miss Julie, he sure hasn't got anything else a young girl like you would want."

"You'd be surprised Velvet, if you really knew." Sarah sat down and ate the meager lunch in front of her.

"You don't eat enough to stay alive on, Miss Julie. I'd rather eat all I want and be fat," Velvet declared as she brought in a glass of buttermilk.

"That's where you're wrong, Velvet. Three months ago I wore a size twenty dress, and was very unhappy and unloved, but today I wear a size twelve, I'm happy, and as for love—well I can take it or leave it."

Velvet helped her get ready for the unveiling, she decided to wear that smooth ultra smart street dress she had bought and the silver mink coat. The dress was a soft blue and her accessories were a shade darker. "M-m-m, Miss Julie, you'll knock their eyes out. Too bad it isn't at night so you could wear an evening gown and show more of yourself."

Sarah admired herself in the mirror. It was still a miracle for her to look into the mirror and see that gorgeous shining creature smiling back at her. "Every time I look at myself, I feel like I've been reincarnated. It's me, and yet it isn't me."

"If I ever got thin again I'd think I'd starved to death and was in heaven," Velvet remarked.

"Talking about food, here is some money, to get the chicken and a few things to go with it. Be sure and fix it like I showed you. I'll probably eat with Mr. Fellows, so you eat some of the chicken. If anyone calls, I'll be back about seven."

At the studio, everything was in an uproar. Fellows hung onto Sarah like she was going to disappear any minute. The audience was noisy and tired of waiting. The majority of them were teen-agers. Helen would probably be there if she were in Chicago, Sarah thought.

The sponsor and the studio manager were conferring on when and how they would present their Mystery Lady. Finally they called Sarah's name, "Miss Le Dere, you're wanted in front." So Sarah and Jim went on stage.

They had rigged up a pedestal for Sarah to stand on. Sarah had worn a veil, and as the men took time to observe her, they both stopped talking and seemed to be incapable of moving. Finally the sponsor, turned to Jim and exclaimed, "Why you never told us that the mystery singer was so beautiful."

"You wanted a mystery didn't you? Well it has been. I just said the lady was shy and didn't want anyone to see her."

They kept watching Sarah as they worked. They had her stand on the pedestal and then they wrapped a large velvet curtain around her. The manager explained, "The pedestal will turn and the velvet will unroll. Then I want you to remove your hat and coat and walk down the runway. We will have a maid take your measurements and we will ask you the information we need, and that's all there is to it. No need to be afraid, Miss Le Dere." He held her arm as he helped her up.

Sarah gave him her sweetest smile and demurely dropped her lashes, as she murmured, "Oh I'm not afraid with all these nice men here."

It was fun standing up there in the dark, hearing the announcer tell about the contest and the rules. And then the voice that said, "And now my dear audience you are about to gaze upon the Mystery Lady you have heard sing so beautifully over your radio."

The big pedestal began turning, and the velvet began to drop away. Slowly and quietly the velvet fell to the floor. Then Sarah realized the pedestal had stopped and she was facing a multitude of faces.

Fellows stood below her in the background, and as she removed her hat and then her coat, she dropped them down into his waiting hands. She began to walk down the flight of stairs, and a spotlight flooded over her. A hush fell over the crowd and for a moment, Sarah felt panicky. Then she started for the runway, and she was startled by the noisy ovation she received. She had never heard so many shrill whistles, yells and applause. It made her blood tingle. She bowed and then threw kisses to all the upturned faces.

The manager came to her rescue and after the noise died down he introduced her, "Ladies and gentlemen, your Mystery

Singer, beautiful, gorgeous, Miss Julie Le Dere." And again the noise engulfed her. She smiled, bowed, waved and threw kisses, but they kept on yelling and whistling. The manager bent and whispered in Julie's ear, "Play a song, that will shut them up."

Julie walked in her best "Miss Baer" manner and went to the piano. She sat down and waited; the noise died away. "Honeysuckle Rose" came from hundreds of throats, so Julie played and sang their favorite number.

Finally the crowd settled down and let the manager and the sponsor interview Julie, take her measurements and picture. "This officially closes our contest, and the ones that are the nearest to Miss Le Dere's lovely, lovely figure and face, will of course be the winners. You will hear from us as soon as we can take care of the millions of letters we have received." He went on and on about their cooperation and support.

Just as the manager rang for the curtain and Julie was taking her last bows, a group of young boys began to crawl up on the stage. They came from all directions. They wanted Julie's autograph. She signed and signed until she was weary, but still they came; young ones, old ones, men, women and stage hands. It was too much, the kids were all right, but most of the men wanted to touch her, paw her. The manager called in a couple of police officers and broke it up. Julie felt dirty and mussed. "Oh, I guess that's what you call being ganged up on."

"Come over here, Julie and sit down a minute. You look exhausted." Jim led her to a chair in an out of the way corner. "After you rest awhile, will you have dinner with me?" He wasn't so talkative today. So far he hadn't had a chance.

Julie wrinkled up her pretty brow, "I guess I'll give you another chance."

He reached out and touched her hand. "Thanks honey, I guess I went off my nut last night, but your face haunts me, even in my sleep."

Julie put her finger to her lips, "S-h-h, don't get started again, Jim."

113

They only had a few seconds of respite, when a call came over the loud speaker, "Miss Julie Le Dere? Are you still here?"

Jim stood up and walked over to the office. He came back and announced, "You'd better look in your mirror and make repairs. Here come the photographers and reporters." He laughed as Julie looked like she wanted to crawl under the chair. "Now don't look so scared, I'll take care of you." He could be nice.

Julie ran a comb quickly through her silvery locks, powdered her nose and put more lipstick on. Checked her eyelashes and smoothed down her dress. "I'm ready, Jim."

Jim motioned to a couple of fellows with cameras. Then two more came up and Jim said, "Gentlemen, Miss Julie Le Dere; this is the Press."

They took pictures from every angle, with her hat and coat on, with them off, standing, sitting, until Julie called quits. They asked her innumerable questions. Julie was a little vague about her past laurels and a little indifferent about the future ones. They found out that Jim Fellows was her manager, and that he had several offers for her. They learned that she was born in Mobile, Alabama; she was an orphan, which was almost true, not counting Mary. She was not married, had no strings attached, was over twenty-one and was very, very beautiful, talented and desirable. "I'd leave home if my old lady would let me, and just follow her around," one of the reporters announced as they walked away. "My boss said, 'Go over and get a quickie of the Mystery Singer.' Wait till he sees these pictures, he'll arrange the whole front page." They laughed and talked about Julie until they separated.

Jim grinned at her, "Well, let's go collect our checks and put on the feed bag. Something tells me, the morning papers are going to be full of Julie Le Dere."

At dinner Jim told Julie about the offer he had, "For three nights a week, you can collect two hundred smackers. You'll sing about four numbers from seven to eight. It's a supper club, with a small orchestra, and a few specialties. Very new, very modern and very smart. They opened about a month ago, and

114

they need a drawing card—bad. I'm sure you would be it," he told her.

"But I'm so unknown." Julie wanted the job, needed the money, and yet she wasn't sure if she would. There was Helen to think of.

Fellows laughed at her remark, "Wait until tomorrow morning, you'll be the breakfast topic."

"How long do they want me?" she asked.

"They offer you a month's engagement for a try-out. But if I know what I think I know, you can write your own ticket." He winked at the lovely bewildered face across the table from him. "Don't worry about it, sleep on it and let me know tomorrow."

Back at the hotel, Julie let Velvet fuss over her, take her coat, hat, help her get into one of those lovely negligees. "O-h-h, you don't know how glad I am to be home. They almost mobbed me tonight." She curled up on the couch and relaxed. "I don't think I'll budge from here, until it's time to go to bed," she declared to the smiling Velvet.

"Well, when I took the chicken down to Mr. Davis, he asked if you planned to be in this evening, and I told him I thought you'd be here for awhile after seven o'clock." She rolled her eyes at Julie.

"So——?" Julie questioned.

"So, Mr. Davis said he would stop on his way out."

"Out where?" She was curious. 'Course Tom was still watching him.

"I don't know, Miss Julie, he didn't enlarge upon the subject."

"Bring me the phone Velvet, please. I want to call long distance."

"Hello darling," Sarah greeted her daughter longingly. "How are you? I'm so lonely, I wish you were here with me."

"If you say so Mother, I'll come right down. I miss you too, but we have been having fun. So many cute boys have come to call."

"Good, I'm glad you're not grieving over Ham." Sarah was relieved.

115

"Oh Mother, I met the sweetest boy—" Helen rambled on. "Daddy hasn't called for days. Is he all right?" She sounded worried.

"Yes, he's fine. I talk to him now and then. He was worrying about the phone bill, so I haven't called him since Saturday."

Sarah had just hung up when the buzzer sounded. It was the manager with the piano. "I'm sorry Miss Le Dere, I didn't have any one to move it until just now," he apologized. He motioned for the men to bring the instrument in. They moved a few pieces of furniture and put it in a corner. "Is that all right, Miss Le Dere?"

Sarah had her hands clasped together like a little girl, her eyer caressing the beautiful object. "Oh yes, it's wonderful, wonderful, thank you very much."

She went to the piano and began singing, "My Sin." Velvet came to the door and listened. When the music stopped, she said softly, "You sound like one of those dark torch singers. I'll bet it gets them." By *them* she meant men.

Sarah went into the bedroom and touched up her face, put some perfume on, admired herself in the mirror and then went back to the piano. She was singing "Deep Purple" when the buzzer sounded.

Velvet went to the door and ushered in George Davis. Sarah went to him with out-stretched hands. "This is a nice surprise, Mr. Davis, thank you so much for the lovely roses." She sat down and invited him to do the same, "Sit here beside me, Mr. Davis, this couch is so comfortable." Funny she didn't feel excited being with him.

"I'm glad you liked the flowers, I thought it was the least I could do after bumping into you last night." He whirled his hat around.

"Velvet, please take Mr. Davis' hat and coat." He handed them to Velvet, still assuring her he hadn't intended to stay. It was strange to be with her own husband when he didn't know it.

Sarah laughed merrily, "Oh if you have some place definite

you want to go, please don't let me detain you." Then she placed her hand on his arm, and said, wistfully, "I had so hoped you would come to see me, this evening." She fluttered her long lashes at him.

The deep red started its upward climb. "Well, if you don't mind, I'd love to spend the evening with you. I was just going to a show." He laughed as he admitted, "I've seen a show most every night for a week." He cast a sheepish look in Sarah's direction. "I heard you playing as I came down the hall." He looked over at the piano.

"Would you like to hear me play?" She looked up at him coyly, "I'd like to play one especially for you." She knew what he was going to ask before he did.

"Do you know 'In the Gloaming'?" He was afraid it would date him.

It wasn't exactly Sarah's kind of song, but she did her best, singing low and softly. Then she sang several others, winding up with, "Haven't We Met Somewhere before?"

She came back and curled up in her corner of the couch. George leaned over and smiled at her, "That was lovely. And that last song reminds me, I have the feeling of having met you before. There's something in your face that haunts me. It's your eyes I think."

Sarah fluttered her lashes, mostly to cover up her pale blue eyes. "I'm afraid that my eyes are very common looking. It's too bad that we haven't met before, though, Mr. Davis." Her voice was swimming in honey.

"Please call me George. I'd like to be considered one of your most devoted admirers. I think you are simply the most beautiful woman I have ever seen, and believe me I've seen my share," he boasted.

Julie closed her eyes, so they wouldn't betray the ugly thought that crossed her mind. "I'll just bet you have, my pet." But to him she said softly, "If I'm to call you 'Jawge,' then you must call me Julie." She held out her little white, soft hand and as

117

George took it in both of his, she added, "I'd like to feel you were really, truly my friend."

Later Velvet served coffee and cake, Julie set the box of chocolates in front of him, and George really enjoyed himself. "That fried chicken your maid brought to me, was the first decent thing I've had since my—my sister left. She went upstate on a vacation."

"Oh, does she keep house for you?" Julie's voice was sweet and guileless. "Oh—so now I'm his sister." Sarah fumed silently.

"Yes Sarah takes care of me and the house. Her daughter Helen is there too." "That makes Helen his niece. How convenient," Sarah thought to herself.

"Oh, then you live here in town?" Sarah pumped him just to see what he'd dream up.

"Yes I have a very lovely home, in the suburbs, on the north-side. I'll have to take you out there some of these days." He still held her hand.

"Gee, that will be nice. It must be wonderful to have a real home of your own. I had one when I was real small I guess, but I've forgotten what it was like." Her tone was sad and bitter.

George squeezed her hand sympathetically, and murmured, "Oh you poor little kid. Don't you have any folks, or sweethearts, or someone that cares?" He was fishing.

Julie dabbed at her eyes with a wisp of a handkerchief, "No, Jawge, I'm all alone. I haven't met a man that I thought I would like for a companion yet." She fluttered her lashes again. George breathed heavily.

"Poor baby." His arm slipped around her slim shoulders.

It was late when he finally tore himself away from her. "I've just got to go, Julie. I've been a meany keeping you up so late, when you should be tucked into bed right now." He kissed her hand tenderly, "I hope I get to see you real soon again." She hung her head shyly, "Would it be too much to ask you to have dinner with me tomorrow night?"

She closed the door softly after he had gone down the hall. Then she let out a whoop of laughter, and Velvet came to the door grinning, "Miss Julie there's one talent you haven't made use of yet."

Sarah giggled, and asked, "And what would that be?"

"The stage; you are a born actress. It won't take many evenings like tonight, before you have him in the palm of your hand."

"I sure hope you're right, Velvet; the quicker the better."

Chapter 14

JULIE AWAKENED TO THE NOISE OF THE BUZZER. SHE HEARD VELVET'S low voice say, "I'm sorry but Miss Le Dere is still asleep. Come back later."

She yawned and stretched contentedly, Velvet peeked in and greeted her mistress. "Good morning, Miss Julie. I hope I didn't wake you up."

"No, Velvet, I just slept myself out, I guess." Oh, the bed felt so nice. She asked sleepily, "Who was at the door just now?"

"A newspaper man, and you have received five bouquets of flowers, two corsages, and a ton of candy." She came back in the room with the morning papers, "Here, you read the news, Miss Julie, while I prepare your breakfast." Then she laughed at Julie's face. "You sure made the headlines this morning." She fixed the pillows behind Julie's back.

Julie's eyes flew over the lines. Georgeous, beautiful, delicious, delectable, bewitching, tantalizing, amazing; those were a few of the adjectives that were used to describe the new sensation, the new Mystery Singer, the lovely, talented Julie Le Dere. Pictures were plastered over the front of every newspaper. After Sarah had gorged herself reading all the nice things that were printed about her, she had her breakfast.

"Gee people make a big stir over the funniest things." She sipped on her second cup of coffee.

"Why you've had more publicity this morning Miss Julie, than the president, or a five star general." She took the tray, "I think it's wonderful."

Velvet drew Julie's bath. After she had dressed she went out to the sitting room. There were flowers everywhere. Velvet had the cards tucked in the top. One from the Banner Soap Company, thanking her again for her grand performance. One from a night club, another from an auto agency. One from Fellows, and one from the Salon where she bought her clothes. The corsages were from George and Grayson. The candy, and there were probably twenty large boxes, came from different stores and clubs in the city. Enough liquor to float a small boat.

"M-m-m, I could go into business. The flowers we'll keep, but the candy must go. It's too much of a temptation. I'll choose a few boxes and mail them to a couple of youngsters I know. This big box of De Metz's I'll keep for Christmas. You can have one Velvet. I'll send Ham one, and my little grocery boy and one for Dora." She sorted out the boxes she wanted to keep, and told Velvet, "Send the rest out to the colored orphanage on Willow Street. I've forgotten the name of it, but you can look it up."

Sarah called George and thanked him for the lovely corsage, a large tiger orchid; brown spots on a pale green background. For someone that was supposed to be an old married man, he certainly had good taste.

Next she called Miss Baer, "This is Julie, your star pupil, remember me?" Velvet was all ears, she hoped she wouldn't have to explain.

Miss Baer was delighted over Sarah's debut into the limelight. "I'm sorry I wasn't here yesterday when you came, but dear I have such a wonderful opening for you. It will only require about two hours of your time in the morning, from ten to noon. A photographer's model." She gave Sarah the address and then went on, "You'll start in the morning. Two hundred dollars a week. He'll need you for about two months. The artist is doing a series of pictures for some magazine."

Sarah stared into the mirror above the table and thanked her

121

pretty face. "Velvet will you please go after something for lunch, I believe I'll invite a guest, if he's not busy."

After Velvet left, Sarah called George, and in Sarah's voice, talked to him for a few minutes. She teased, "You don't sound so grumpy this morning dear, what's happened?"

"Oh I met some fellows in the hotel, and we've been playing cards and shooting pool."

"Well I'm glad, I was sort of worried about you. I might not get back until the holidays, George."

"Don't bother about me, Sarah, I'll be all right."

"How about the restaurant food, does it agree with you?" She just had to keep the laughs out of her voice.

"Oh I get a good meal once in awhile." Yes, whenever Julie feeds you, Sarah thought. She promised to call him during the week-end. He wasn't too anxious to talk to her or was it just her imagination? He hadn't even asked about Helen.

After she finished talking to George, she called Bob Grayson. "No, I'm not busy, Julie. I'd love to come to lunch."

Then the phone rang right after she had hung up from her conversation with Bob. She answered, "Oh, it's you Jim."

"Yes, your line has been busier than a telephone switchboard," he complained. "I called earlier, but your Great Dane wouldn't let me talk to you. Say, Julie, I've got some hot news. Have you read the papers yet?"

"Yes, Jim, all of them," she laughed.

"I told you, didn't I, you'd be plastered all over the front pages? Beautiful blonde rescued by the police. Gorgeous Julie mobbed by audience. Some publicity, huh?"

"People don't believe everything they read in the papers, do they?" This was rather distasteful to Sarah, but very necessary to Julie.

"Some people do. The offer I told you about yesterday, is much better; they now offer you three hundred a week. Better take it, Julie; keep yourself in the public's eye."

"If you think it's all right, I'll take it, Jim."

"Good, I'll call you back after I make all the arrangements."

122

Lunch was ready and waiting when Bob made his appearance. Velvet became his abject slave right from the first moment. She told Julie later, "Now if I were in your shoes, Miss Julie, I'd take out after him."

"He is nice, and such a marvelous dancer, but he still isn't what I want."

Velvet shook her head, and carried out the remains of the luncheon. Sarah curled up on the couch and thought about Bob. He hadn't said too much verbally, but his eyes, his actions had said it for him. He had asked for a date, and she had promised to go dancing with him the next night. "I could fall for him, like a ton of bricks, but I can't. It would break Helen's heart, and I'm not going to permit her Mother to do it." And Sarah knew in her heart she was ringing the curtain down on a romance that happens once in a lifetime, killed it before it even started. Sarah might have had mad ideas and foolish plans; Julie might have fame and glory; but Helen's mother would stay the same.

Chapter 15

THE BEAUTIFUL JULIE WAS DRESSED IN A SEA FOAM GREEN CHIFFON gown with George's perfect orchid pinned to her shoulder. She wore emeralds and diamonds. When George walked in the door, he could only smile and stare. Finally he blurted out, "You look like a shining star. I never knew anyone so beautiful." He couldn't take his eyes off her face, he walked to the couch and sank down on it, without realizing he was doing it. He was spellbound.

Julie laughed gaily, "Please don't let my flash of fame blind you, Jawge. The public soon forgets you." It eased the situation, and George regained his composure.

"By jove, you really were the talk of the town this morning. Everywhere I went, the barber shop, the pool room, the gym, that's all you heard. Julie Le Dere, the haunting beauty." They both laughed.

"I didn't know you were athletic." H-m-m-p, so now he's going in for exercises.

George's face took on its usual pink tinge. "Got to watch the waist line." He patted his tummy.

Julie's eyes went over his impressive figure. He didn't look bad in his evening clothes, in fact, he looked the part of a "rich sugar daddy." She giggled inside. She bet he had gone home and picked up his suit. It needed pressing when she put it away. No doubt he had called in the hotel valet to help him. He was so helpless.

"Velvet get me my wrap, please. Where shall we go Jawge?"

George helped her up, and smiled down at her upturned face, "Wherever your majesty wishes."

"Oh now, Jawge, please don't treat me like I'm something special. I'm still little Julie. How about the College Inn?"

Velvet brought the white ermine out and George took it from her and wrapped Julie up to her ears in it. "It's pretty cold out tonight, supposed to snow. We'll have a White Christmas after all."

"Gee, Christmas is only a week off." Julie bit her lips, "White Christmas for you, and a Blue Christmas for me." Her voice broke with sadness. "If it wasn't for my dear Velvet, I'd be all alone."

George cleared his throat and got out a couple of "H-m-m-p's," then he said, tenderly, "Don't you worry your beautiful little head about it. You'll have a wonderful Christmas if old George has anything to do with it." He chucked her under her chin.

Julie flashed her smoky blue eyes at him, indignantly. "Don't you dare call my Jawge old. You're just at the right age to enjoy living."

"I've been waiting for you to come along. You really don't think I'm too old for you?" His faded brown eyes regarded her seriously.

Julie grabbed his arm and steered him towards the door. "Of course not, silly, I wouldn't change you for the world." George squeezed her closer to him.

The College Inn had a wonderful floor show, they had a grand dinner, which of course, Julie only picked at. They danced; waltzes, fox-trots, and two steps. The orchestra played a rumba and Julie tapped the table in time to the music. "Do you know how to rumba, Jawge?"

"No, Julie, I'm sorry."

"Never mind sugar, I'll teach you, tomorrow, don't forget."

The Master of Ceremonies singled Julie out, turned the spotlight on her and announced her presence among them. She had to stand up and take a bow. George smirked at all the men that gave her a big hand.

"I almost have to carry a club when I go out with you, Julie."

They came home in a cab. Julie invited him in. It was midnight, but she wanted to get in a few good punches before she let him go. So far everything had gone along fine, but time was running out.

"Come on, Jawge I'll make you some coffee, or would you prefer a night cap? Some liquor store sent me a case of mixed liquors."

"Good, we'll sample some of it." George laid his coat on a chair and helped Julie remove hers. He remarked, "This is a lovely coat, must have cost you plenty."

Julie answered nonchalantly, "I suppose so, it was given to me last Christmas by a very dear friend."

George hefted the coat then laid it on top of his. "H-m-m-p, must have cost a fortune. What do you want for Christmas this year?"

Julie had gone to a little cupboard packed full of liquor and glasses. She smiled up at George as she answered flippantly, "Oh I want a big blue Buick. I've just got to have a car some way." Then she picked up a bottle of three star brandy. "Will this do?"

"Fine, just fine." He took the bottle from her and opened it, poured two small drinks into the glasses. Then he held his up and looked long into her heavily fringed eyes. "To the most beautiful woman in the world. Julie, I'd give a lot if I could have met you long before." He drank his brandy and set it down. His voice sounded strained and frustrated.

Julie smiled to herself—filled his glass again and followed him to the couch. She set his glass on the coffee table. "One little drink isn't enough for a big man like you, Jawge." Julie sipped her fiery drink slowly. "Do you play cards, Jawge?"

"Love to, poker, rummy, everything. Do you?" He picked up her little soft hand.

126

"Oh I love to gamble. We'll have to have a poker session some evening."

"How about tomorrow night—unless you have other plans."

"Yes Jawge, I have a dinner date. But Jawge," she sidled up to him, "I want you to come tomorrow afternoon and take your dancing lesson. If we're going dancing, you've got to know how to do all the latest steps." She laid her silvery head on his shoulder, and added hastily, "Not that you don't dance divinely now, but you should keep up with the latest steps."

"With you as my teacher, I'll try anything," George promised heartily.

"Do you ride?" Julie thought about old Dobbin, and giggled.

"Horseback? Oh I'm crazy about it. Do you?" His arm slowly encircled her shoulders.

"Oh yes, Jawge, let's go some morning." She closed her eyes and snuggled closer in the curve of his arm. The long black lashes lay on her slightly pink cheeks. Her mouth was like a red rose bud. Julie held her breath, feeling George's heart pumping like an overworked engine.

Then, George bent his head and gently kissed her. Julie's eyes fluttered open and she whispered, "Oh, Jawge should you?" Her eyes were filled with gray mysterious shadows.

"Oh yes, little Julie, I must." His lips closed over hers again.

"Oh Jawge you kiss so divinely." Then Julie stood up and held out her hands, "Come darling, you must go home now." Her smile was provocative.

"Must I, sweetheart?" he pleaded.

"Yes sugar you must. Call me in the morning. I have to model for an artist in the morning, but I'll be back for lunch." Her voice was filled with excitement, "We'll lunch together and then I'll give you your dancing lesson. We can be together all afternoon."

George's face lit up like a hundred bulb light. "Swell Julie, I'll be here." He picked up his coat and went to the door. Julie following, he opened the door and stood waiting.

Julie moved closer and his arms reached out and pulled her

close to him, "I hate to say good night, but I must." His eyes searched hers.

"You must, Jawge." His head bent to meet hers and Julie returned his kiss with just the right amount of feeling. He held her close for a moment then went down the hall. She wondered —Sarah Davis wondered—how many hadn't insisted.

Julie closed the door and took a couple of quick steps around the room, "I've got him hook, line, and sinker. I'll have him wrapped up and tied by Christmas eve," she promised herself.

Velvet came out and took Julie's coat and asked softly, "Seems to me you're making headway Miss Julie."

Julie flashed her a happy smile, "I've got him on the run now."

Velvet chuckled, "If that's what you want, I'm right behind you pushing."

"I'd better get to sleep, I've got to look pretty in the morning."

Julie started her modeling career off with a bang; the photographer was fascinated with her beauty. "I've painted and photographed thousands of girls, Miss Le Dere, and I must say you have an almost fatal beauty. An elusive something that I hope I can capture with the camera. Helen of Troy had it, Josephine and many other famous beauties." Julie smiled her thank you. "Has anyone told you that you have a haunting resemblance to Jean Harlow?"

"Many times. I just hope I have a better ending than she did," Julie confided.

"I imagine you'll always have men trouble. That's the curse of beauty; the wolves won't leave you alone," he told her as he arranged his cameras. "Oh by the way, you can come in every other day, for awhile."

He had Julie put on a costume, beautiful but scanty. At first she felt embarrassed and ill at ease, but while he was adjusting the lenses and lights, she convinced herself it was what she had to expect. And besides, Miss Baer had told her he was a perfect gentleman.

The phone rang just as he was ready to shoot. "Helen, yes,

she's here. Perfectly satisfied. I could kiss you, I couldn't have done better myself."

Naturally that was Miss Baer calling about her. Julie felt a warm glow of pride.

It was rather tiresome, and hot, but she had done harder things than posing and having her picture taken. On the whole she felt she had landed in a pretty soft spot.

Chapter 16

GEORGE WAS WAITING FOR HER WHEN SHE ARRIVED AT THE APART-
ment. Velvet had fixed him a drink, and he was in a good mood.
Julie swept in, bringing a fresh perfumed wind with her. "Brr—
it's so cold out sugar. How are you?" She went to him and gave
him a quick light kiss.

George's face took on an apoplectic red. "Shall I fix you a
drink, Julie?" He busied himself at the cupboard.

"Please Jawge. I'll change if you'll excuse me for a second,"
Julie murmured as she went on into the bedroom. Velvet helped
her make a quick change. She put on a low necked white bolero
blouse and a pair of black velvet slacks, with a red sash wound
around and around her tiny waist.

George turned with the glasses as she came back in. He
grinned at her cute shape so revealing in the soft velvet. "Oh
you look charming."

Inside Julie, Sarah fumed, "Liar, you know how you hate
women in slacks, unless of course it was just me." To George,
Julie answered, like a happy child, "Do you really like them,
darlin'?"

He handed a drink to her and they walked to the other side
of the room. "You're about as big as a bug," George remarked.

"I just look that way, because you're so tall and strong." Julie's
eyes travelled over George's slightly corpulent body.

"Well how did the modeling job go?" He took her free hand.

"Wonderful, Mr. Reddin is so nice." She closed her eyes as she pretended to be reminiscent about her mornings contacts. "Very nice."

"H-m-mp, so it's getting colder out?" She nodded her head, lazily, contentedly. "Comfortable, little one?" George whispered in her ear.

"This is my idea of heaven." Julie's narrow shadowed eyes caressed him, teasingly.

"Is he young and handsome?" George carefully set his glass on the coffee table.

Julie waited a minute and then innocently asked, "Who's young?"

George squeezed her hand, "This artist, Mr. Reddin."

"Oh yes, very nice and unusually good looking, so young and full of fire." She giggled inside, "Why I believe he's getting jealous."

She got up and went to the piano, George trailed after her and draped himself over the instrument. Julie played "Jealousy" and sang it in a tantalizing way.

George grinned and nodded his head. "Can't help it, Julie, a man doesn't meet a woman like you every day." He bent and kissed the soft spot in her neck.

Julie's hands flew to her throat, "Jawge, that was naughty." Her eyes dropped demurely.

"I'm sorry honey, but you tempt me beyond endurance." He ran his hand over her shoulder.

It gave Julie the cold shivers, "M-m-m, he never used this technique on me before." Silently Sarah Davis warned, "Control yourself, George, I might be beautiful, but I'm good." She walked away from him. "Velvet is lunch ready?" Velvet called back, "Almost Miss Julie."

George came up and slipped his arms around her waist. He held her against his chest. "I've made you angry. I'm sorry Julie, but I'll do it again if I get the chance." He bit the tip of her pink ear. "I wish I had the right to do all the things that have been going through my mind."

Julie whirled away from him, "Jawge you frighten me. If we were engaged or had an understanding, perhaps I could overlook these advances." She looked up into his tortured eyes. "In fact I think I'd kind of like it."

His arms pulled her to him. "Oh my God, if I could figure out some way——" She looked at him as he went on, "First time in my life I wanted something I couldn't have." He nearly squeezed the breath out of her.

"Why Jawge, I didn't know you really cared. If you're real good, I might see what I can do." Her promise was a little vague. She laughed to herself, "I'll bet he's wishing Sarah would drop dead or something."

After lunch, which George relished very much, they picked out the records they liked and Julie began giving George some inside information on the behavior of the hips. She danced in front of him, giving him the general idea of the rumba. Then he tried it with her. Julie cried out gaily, "Watch my hips Jawge, watch the way I move them," she instructed him.

"I'm not missing anything, Julie my sweet," George assured her.

"Don't you just love it?" Julie asked him, as they moved their bodies to the rumba's beat.

"M-m-m, crazy about it." George pulled her to him.

"No Jawge, you can't do it so close together." She pushed him back.

"But I like to dance close to you," he pouted.

"Let's try a tango now." Julie ran to the record machine and changed the music.

The strains of "I Get Ideas" came to them. George took her in his arms, Julie started to sing, "I get ideas, m-m-m," and so on.

George laughed and whispered loudly in her ear, "I've already got them pet." It was plain his mind wasn't on dancing.

"That's all for today, Jawge. We'll have a drink and then you must go. I have to dress for tonight."

132

"Oh Julie can't you ditch the other guy and go somewhere with me. I'm so lonely." He looked ridiculous, when he pulled that little boy act.

"I just can't do that, Jawge. Mr. Grayson wouldn't like it."

"Who's he?" He was mixing the drinks.

"Bob? Oh he's a very good friend. A wonderful dancer."

The phone rang and Julie hurried to answer it. She hoped it wasn't Helen. It was Tom Masters.

"Tom, I have some things for you to do, but I'll have to call you back later." Julie hung up and joined George in a drink.

"Who is Tom?" His face was a mile long.

"Tom? Oh he's my agent and sometimes my body guard," Julie informed him.

They sipped on the drinks, not talking, when the phone rang again.

It was Jim Fellows. "Hey Julie, you will begin tomorrow night at seven. Prepare four numbers. Duck soup. A high dive. Class. You'll like it, good food, nice guy to work for, hot orchestra, colored. I'll pick you up about six bells. We'll go early so you can get briefed."

Julie hung up and went back to the couch.

George growled, "Who's Jim?"

"He's my Chicago manager, Jawge. Nice fellow." He was burning, she laughed silently. Poor George, he always had to be the big cheese.

He set his drink down and said, "Well, I guess I better make way for the next one."

"Oh sugar you don't mean that." Julie huddled down in the soft pillows. "I didn't know you would want to take me out tonight." Her mouth quivered like a spanked child's.

George coughed, "H-m-m-p, well, of course I have no right to expect you to give up all your other friends." He walked towards the door.

Julie glided to his side ."Would you like me to, Jawge?" The southern honey poured all over him.

"Would I? But—" He took her in his arms, and looked deep

133

into the long narrow teasing eyes. "Oh Julie, if I only could." He kissed her waiting lips and went out the door.

Velvet came in softly, and stood there looking at Miss Julie doubling over with laughter. "Oh, Velvet, I've never had so much fun in my life." She fell into a chair and wiped her eyes. "I never dreamed men were such gullible fools."

"Miss Julie, they've been that way ever since Eve got Adam to eat the apple." Velvet smiled wisely at the girl curled up in the big chair. "The older you get Miss Julie, the more you'll understand what I'm talking about." Velvet went over and picked up the empty glasses. "Will you want anything to eat, before you go out Miss Julie?"

"No, I'll eat out, but you had better order something for your supper. If you have anything you want to do, please feel free to go out, Velvet. I won't be back till late, and I can put myself to bed." And she thought, it's almost forty years I've been tucking myself in. She smiled to think what Velvet would say if she knew how old she really was.

Chapter 17

MORNING CAME AND JULIE WAS SLIGHTLY UNDER THE WEATHER. Velvet informed her with, "Ah, it seems to me, Miss Julie, that you have something occupying your pretty head, that you didn't have yesterday."

"What's that, Velvet?" she moaned.

"A hangover, honeychild." Velvet went about fixing her up like an old veteran. "You're not used to drinking, are you?" she asked the tossing Julie.

"Oh, no, never knew what it tasted like until a couple of weeks ago," she admitted.

"Then if you'll take my advice, Miss Julie, you'll stick to soda water. You got to sing tonight." Velvet draped an ice bag over Julie's silver curls. A hot water bottle on the flat stomach. Alka-Seltzer inside the flat stomach. "There now, just lie still and forget you're living," the practical maid advised.

Door bells buzzed, telephones rang, but Velvet ruled with an iron hand. "Sorry Miss Julie is indisposed at the moment, call back later." "Come back later," and so on for several hours.

About eleven o'clock Julie felt like getting up. Cold tomato juice and hot black coffee helped a lot. "Oh never again will I be so foolish." She sat with her head in her hands.

"That's what they call 'the famous last words,' Miss Julie.

But for your voice and career as model, I hope you mean it. Liquor can spoil your looks awfully fast."

"I never drank before and there's no need for me to do it now. The next time we have guests, Velvet, you mix the drinks, and just give me water."

"Do you feel well enough to attend to business Miss Julie?" Velvet's modulated voice was sympathetic.

"Can't let it pile up, can we, Velvet?" Julie tried to look interested. "Fire away, commander," she ordered.

"First Mr. Davis called. He wants to come down and see you. Thinks he can help. Then Mr. Masters called. Mr. Grayson called. You have several important looking letters. A bouquet of flowers from Mr. Davis. A gift from Mr. Grayson. I think it's a book. A corsage from Mr. Fellows. It must be wonderful to be young and beautiful, Miss Julie." Velvet fussed around her pillows.

Julie sighed happily, "Oh it is wonderful, I can't get used to it."

Velvet glanced at her with a question on her lips, but it remained unspoken. Julie was reading a letter with a happy smile on her face. "Oh Velvet, the radio station wants me back to broadcast daily for a new program. Wheee, get me my clothes, I feel like a new woman." She sprang out of bed.

Julie called Helen before she did anything else. "Darling girl, how are you? Did you and Jerry get the candy? What do you want for Christmas? A nice fur coat? Okay, I'll see what I can do." Julie hung up and then waited a few minutes and called George.

"Hello George, Sarah," in Sarah's dull, uninspired middle western voice. "Thought I'd better call you dear, and see how you're getting along. Just one more week—then Christmas. Have you thought about what you want to get Helen? No—well she wants a nice fur coat, yes I said a fur coat. Oh I don't know dear—I think we can afford it. Oh, I'd suggest a sheared beaver, or perhaps a short seal coat. Whatever you decide will be fine.

136

Me? Oh I'd rather wait and get me a new car." She hoped he wouldn't have a stroke over their expensive requests.

After she had called Tom Masters and given him peculiar orders such as a flash bulb camera, and an invitation to her table at the club, a call to Grayson; her voice conveying her feelings towards him; then George, the unsuspecting victim, the innocent lamb to be sheared. In that southern accent that stirred him so, "Jawge, darling, have you had your lunch? Good, do you have any plans for this afternoon? No, suppose you come down and go shopping with me? Sick? Oh, I'm much better."

Julie had to go talk to the manager of the radio station. She accepted his offer to sing every afternoon, on a fifteen minute program, one song to open it and one to sign off with, a hundred dollars a week. But Jim Fellows wasn't in on the deal. It would all be gravy after Christmas, when she was living at home again. Then they went shopping.

First Julie steered George to a perfume counter. There she suggested he buy certain odors for the sister he had mentioned. "Give her a little beauty in her life." George laughed, "If you only knew Sarah. She's such an old maid, never wears make-up, or dresses up to date. Old fashioned and a homebody, that's my sister." George smelled all the bottles Julie pointed out to him. "Well, if you insist I'll get her some." The saleslady wanted thirty dollars for a small bottle. George nearly exploded, but because Julie had her adoring gaze fixed on him, he paid it. Then he even bought her a bottle. "I might as well do it up brown. I think I'll get a bottle for my niece too." So Julie helped him pick something out that was suitable for a young girl.

"I'm sure her mother will approve of this. It's light and flowery." Then she turned her fluttering lashes on George and whispered, "And I'm just wild over my gift, darling." She hooked her arm in his. "I want to get me a riding habit, Jawge, I left my other one in Hollywood. It had seen its best days."

She came out all dressed in her riding suit, cap and boots. "How do I look darling? All I need now is the horse."

From there they wandered into the fur salon. "Oh, I just love furs, but I have so many coats now." Julie went straight to a flaring short coat, "Oh Jawge look at this adorable coat. I'll bet your niece would look sweet in this." The saleslady had Julie slip it on. In her best Domere strut she showed George how Helen would look in it. "Can't you just see her dear little face peeking out between these huge lapels?"

George put his glasses on and fingered the fur. "H-m-m-p, looks pretty good." He peeked at the price tag. "By jove they want three hundred for this dyed rabbit." He dropped the tag like it burned his fingers. "Too much money. I did want to see something in a fur coat, but not that high," he informed the saleswoman.

Julie puckered up her lips, "But Jawge, this is just right for a young lady Helen's age. This is lovely fur, sheared beaver." Julie smoothed the thick fur with her tiny jeweled hand.

George's eyes followed her little white hand as it moved. "H-m-m-p, a man has to be careful, Julie. I think the world of Helen, but there's a limit to everything." He looked at the coat the saleslady held up.

"Oh that's much too old and heavy for a young child. How old did you say she was Jawge?" Julie looked closely at the coat. She knew Helen would despise it.

"She's seventeen. No I don't think that's suitable." He looked at the different models around the room. Julie dancing after him, still in the short sheared beaver. Julie frowned on all the coats the woman showed them. Helen just had to get the one she had on, even if she had to pay for it herself. Finally George shrugged his shoulders and gave in, "Okay I'll take the sheared beaver. Are you sure, Julie, it's suitable for a young girl?" He took his checkbook out and wrote the amount on it and handed it to the saleslady.

"Do you want it sent out sir?"

"Yes send it to the Lawrence Hotel."

Julie turned to him and made a kiss with her lips, "Oh Jawge I wish I had a wonderful uncle like you."

He smiled down on her, "But I don't want to be just an uncle to you."

They walked down a boulevard that just happened to have the Buick agency tucked between the tall buildings. When they approached the big show windows, Julie gave out a little excited cry. She ran to the window and pressed her nose against the cold pane. "Oh Jawge, if little Julie could have that for Christmas, she'd really think there was a Santa Claus." She spoke in an awed whisper. "Isn't it beautiful?" She barely breathed the words.

George peered in the window too. "Costs about thirty-three hundred the way it stands. You don't need Santa Claus, you need a banker."

Julie pressed her body against George's, and she murmured, "A banker, M-m-m, maybe I could find a banker someday." Her eyes appraised him coolly, weighing him against "the banker."

George coughed, and laughed, "No sense in standing here, let's go in and look at it." It didn't cost anything to look, he argued to himself.

The salesman met them bowing and smiling. George explained they wanted to look at the blue special in the window. Naturally Julie wanted to sit behind the wheel, and then a crowd gathered. The salesman said, "Aren't you Miss Le Dere—the one who's on everybody's lips these days?"

"Yes I am." Julie wasn't interested in the salesman. She was steering the big car, blowing the horn and ahhing, and ohhing. "Oh Jawge, it is so beautiful, just what I want."

"It's not half as lovely as you dear. And it's much too big for you Julie, you can't see to drive it." George tried to discourage her.

"Oh we have a special pillow and an adjustment for short people," the salesman hurried to assure them. George glared at him.

"Oh well I can dream, can't I." Julie's voice was tired and very disappointed. "I guess I'll have to hunt my banker up," she threatened.

139

They arrived home, Julie giving George her hand at the door, "Thanks for going with me." He held on to her hand.

"Can't I come in, I've shared you with the public all day." George's red face looked crestfallen.

"I'm sorry, Jawge, but I sing tonight, and I want to rest before I dress. Perhaps tomorrow Jawge." But her voice scared him, he felt the skids under him.

"Oh Julie don't be so mean to me, please." It did her heart good to hear him beg. "No, not tonight," and she slipped in the door and closed it.

George walked slowly down the hall.

"I don't know what you're working for, but I recognize the signs. Do you think it's going to work, Miss Julie?" Velvet was a highly interested party.

"I don't know—I'm shooting for a nice big shiny Buick." Julie kicked her shoes off and started to undress. "I'll have my bath and then I'm going to just lie here and rest. I do not wish to be disturbed, Velvet."

"I understand Miss Julie, but what if he brings the Buick up here?"

"He won't." Velvet helped her into the tub. "I think I'll wear that strapless black velvet tonight, Velvet, and lots of diamonds."

Jim Fellows was almost speechless when Julie made her entrance. She had his corsage pinned low, on the pencil slim gown; creamy white camellias. "Thanks Jim for the lovely flowers."

"I wish I were able to send them to you every day. Say that's some gown, you'll knock them dead."

Julie looked down at the sheath of velvet. "One time I wondered how a person could keep one of these strapless creations on, now I know—with a prayer."

Fellows laughed and let his gaze linger on Julie's coke bottle shape. "You shouldn't have any trouble."

Velvet brought out the ermine. Over the black, it was very arresting. "Shall we go, Jim?"

140

"Be careful, Miss Julie, and don't crush your flowers," Velvet warned.

George was just entering the lobby when Julie and her escort were leaving. Julie flashed him a teasing smile. George removed his hat and bowed. When he looked up, she was gone in a cloud of exhaust smoke.

"H-m-m-p, so that's the big date." He growled at the elevator boy. "Tenth." Oh well he could use some sleep. He was too old to stay up every night, but——

George didn't go to sleep, he lay there for hours going over the same problems. He could ask Sarah for a divorce, but then what about Helen? What grounds would he give? Sarah was a perfect wife, good, kind, loyal. She would get all the property, money and Helen. No—what if she died, but how? What if she got run over, or hit by a car, but by whom, or how? No, if Sarah got all the money, and the property, Julie wouldn't want him either. Everything she wanted cost money, lots of it. He'd have to give Helen up, she wouldn't have him for a father if he didn't want her Mother anymore. And if she found out he was running around with a beautiful model or singer, a celebrity, Helen would hate him, and Sarah would have plenty of grounds to divorce him and take everything. Illinois laws were unfair to husbands, he thought rebelliously. She wanted that Buick so bad, and if he didn't give it to her she would find someone that would and could.

George crawled out of bed and poured himself a drink, then he poured another one, and another one. Then he called Velvet. "What time will Miss Julie be back?" "About ten o'clock." George was slightly tipsy when he knocked on Julie's door.

"Velvet I want to come in and wait for Miss Julie." He weaved just the least bit, in his effort to be impressive. He took a five dollar bill from his wallet, he held it up temptingly.

"I don't know if I should Mr. George. But if you insist—" Velvet's fingers latched onto the bill. "Come in Mr. George and make yourself at home. You know where the liquor is kept." She watched him make his way over to the cupboard. He poured

141

himself a stiff one. Velvet disappeared in the back of the apartment.

George played some records and moped. What a girl. Beauty, beauty and so much of it, and brains. Once in a lifetime. Oh God, if he only knew what to do. He slumped down on the couch, his head cradled in his hands. "I haven't got a chance with three females against me. I wonder if I could persuade her to live in another city."

George's eyes glowed with hope. He poured another drink, it seemed a pretty good idea. Then he thought of the lies he'd have to tell, to Julie, to Helen and Sarah. The expense of two homes, the longing for one and the dislike of the other. The wear and tear on his nerves. The good food Sarah served, the beauty Julie offered. "M-m-m, what shall I do. Give her up, forget her, how can I?"

Julie found a muddled and confused man when Velvet let her in. "Mr. George wanted to see you tonight Miss Julie, and I thought it might be important." She emphasized the words. She took Julie's coat and faded from the room.

Julie rubbed her hands. It was awfully cold outside. Her teeth were chattering not altogether with the cold, George looked so formidable, and just a wee bit drunk. Sarah had an abhorrence for drunks. Julie was a little frightened, as George stood up and came to her.

"Julie, my beautiful one. I've been worrying all night what I'm going to do about you. I can't give you up, yet at this time it's impossible for me to make any plans." That's what he needed was time. His arms encircled her.

Julie ducked her head, his breath was so powerful, it almost floored her, "Please Jawge, you've been drinking." She tried to push him away but he pulled her closer.

"Oh darling, don't treat me so mean. I'll buy you the Buick, Julie, I'll go with you in the morning and we'll get it. I want you to have it for Christmas."

"Oh Jawge, don't make me laugh, you're so drunk you'll forget it by morning. You'd better go now." She tried again to get out

142

of his tight embrace. She threw her head back and looked at him with teasing, doubting eyes. "Jawge, please."

"No, Julie, I'm not going to let you go, now or ever. There's too many men waiting for you. No, I'm going to buy you that Buick." He held on to her with one hand and dug in his pocket for his check book. "I'll show you!" He gave her the book, "Make out a check to that Buick agency, thirty-two hundred dollars. O-h-h, that's a lot of money, but Julie my sweet you're worth it. Here let me sign it. Now you keep the check and we'll go after it bright and early." He made a magnanimous gesture. "Oh, what's money."

Julie held the check; a new Buick, it was unbelievable. And he had said, "We can't afford a new car Sarah." Julie laughed deep down. She was still Sarah inside. "Jawge you've made me happier than I've been in my life. You've really surprised me, Jawge." She guided him to the door, "Please go now, Jawge, I'm so happy I want to cry." She put her arms around his neck and kissed him sweetly, passionately and lovingly, and then she pushed him out into the hall. "Good night darlin'." She watched him walk uncertainly down the hall. She hoped he found his room all right. She sat down in a chair, still looking at the check.

Velvet tip-toed into the room, "I thought I heard the door close."

"Yes, Velvet, Mr. Davis went back upstairs." She waved the check laughing, "Here's my new Buick, Velvet. It wasn't as hard to get as I thought it would be." Julie's eyes were calculating and cold. "I just never had the proper tools to use before."

"I've never seen a man yet that a good looking woman couldn't just wrap right around her finger, anytime she wanted to," Velvet declared.

"How right you are, Velvet." She walked into the bedroom and carefully placed it in her bag. "This is one of the biggest, nicest Christmas presents I've ever gotten." She smiled at the beautiful woman in the mirror. "Thanks to you," she murmured.

After she was tucked in bed, Julie propped herself up with the soft fluffy pillows and meditated. "What if George figures out a way to get rid of Sarah and proposes marriage?" she asked herself. "Oh, but he wouldn't because he knows Sarah would get everything, including Helen, and he couldn't bear being separated from her." She really had him over a barrel. But supposing he did ask Sarah for a divorce. M-m-m, he couldn't offer Julie very much then, just his salary and a few bonds. "Then I just wouldn't have him, I'd give him the cold shoulder." She stared at the wall awhile thinking, "What if he drops me like a cold potato when Sarah tells him she's coming back?" She giggled, "I'll have to get some good evidence on him, and then I'll sue him for alienation of affections."

Her mind kept figuring out every angle she could think up. "Maybe I could kill Sarah off, or have her get a divorce away from here. I'd have to have a reason. M-m-m, I could have Helen call her Daddy and tell him that Mrs. Sangster saw him out with some show girl and ask him what it's all about and have her lay the law down to him." Julie snuggled down in the pillows. "I'll wait until Monday or so, then I'll tell her to call him. I can just see his face now, denying it. But I'll wait until I have the Buick. At least I can prove that I wheedled something out of him, and wrapped him around my little finger, once in my life." A smile of satisfaction played on her lips. "Well, I'll just go along until the first of the week and let things work out by themselves."

She fixed her pillows and lay down preparing to go to sleep, but sleep just wouldn't take over. Her mind was as busy as the Grand Central Station. "What if he doesn't like me anymore, after he finds out what I've done? What if he decides he wants Sarah back and won't have me? What if he doesn't want a gorgeous wife?" Julie sniffed, "H-m-m-p, well then I know somebody that does."

144

Chapter 18

VELVET CALLED JULIE AT EIGHT, "I KNOW YOU'RE ANXIOUS TO GET started. That Buick is just sitting there waiting for you, Miss Julie."

"Gee I hope it is. Oh well if it isn't I'll just order another one." She was having her breakfast when George called. Julie told Velvet to tell him to come on down and have coffee.

When he arrived, Julie offered him her free hand, "Good morning, dear, sit down and have some delicious hot cakes."

He smiled tenderly at her and then looked at Velvet and said, "There's nothing better than hot cakes on a cold morning." After Velvet left, he looked at Julie's fresh lovely face and added softly, "Unless it's a beautiful woman."

She smiled back at him and cautioned, "Can't live on love, Jawge, or beauty. Money is the main thing in my life. With it you can do most everything, without it, you're just a lost duck." She peeked through the heavy fringes she called lashes.

He sighed, "Yeah I guess you're right. If a man has money, he can buy anything he wants." He looked at her with calculating eyes.

Julie answered that crack by saying, "Within reason of course. You're not sorry you gave me the check are you Jawge?" Her heart took a nose dive with fear, but he laughed softly and patted her hand resting on the table.

145

"No darling, I want you to have the Buick if that's what you want. I guess I owe you something for all the nice times I've spent down here, and putting up with me when I drink too much." He leaned over and looked deep into her eyes, "I'm sorry I was tight last night. You're sweet Julie."

They arrived at the agency just as the doors were opened. The Buick was still available. Julie was thrilled to pieces. "Oh-h-h, I just can't believe that gorgeous thing is going to be mine." She squeezed George's arm. "Oh, you're a honey, Jawge."

The salesman ushered them into the office. "It will be all yours as soon as we can make out the bill of sale and all the necessary papers."

George drove the new car to the studio where Julie had to model. "I'll go back to the hotel and wait for you. Do you want me to come after you?"

"No, I'll take a cab, Jawge, there's no place to park down here. Please be careful of my blue baby Jawgie." Julie kissed him sweetly and jumped out of the luxurious car. She waved as he moved away. "Poor dear, he doesn't know he's driving his own car."

Back at the hotel Velvet had a good hot lunch waiting for her. "Don't you have to go to the radio station this afternoon, Miss Julie?"

"No, not until Monday afternoon. Did you call Mr. Jawge, Velvet?" Julie asked as she removed her mink coat.

"Yes'm, he said he'd be right down. Did you get the car?" The maid's face was shining with pleasure for her beautiful mistress.

"Oh yes, and it's out of this world." "Especially compared to the old gray antique," she thought. "I let Mr. Jawge drive it back to the hotel. I haven't driven it yet, but maybe we'll go out this afternoon."

George came in and joined her for lunch. Julie asked, "Jawge darlin', do you have your riding clothes here?"

"No, darling, they are out at the house. Why?" His pale brown eyes regarded her with a sick calf's look.

"Oh I just thought it's so bright and sunny out, it would be a

146

grand day for a ride. Besides, sugar, I want to try out my new habit." Julie sidled up to him and puckered up her lips, "Please, darlin'."

How could he refuse such a beautiful face?" "Okay sweet, but we'll have to go out to my house first."

"Swell then you can show me all around. And I'll let you drive my new car." She put her arm around his waist and hugged him. "I'll be ready in a jiffy."

"You know Julie I ought to take those gifts out there with me." He talked loudly so she could hear him.

From the bedroom came Julie's sweet southern drawl advising him, "Oh no, Jawge, you better let me help you wrap them first. We'll do that some evening and then we can take them out." Silence and then she asked innocently, "When are you expecting them back, Jawge?"

"I talked to Sarah yesterday and she thought they'd be home for Christmas eve. I'll have to get a tree and trim it."

Julie cried, "Oh let me help, Jawge, that will be so much fun."

George drove out to the northwest side of town, slowly and carefully. "Can't drive too fast, Julie, when it's so new. Have to break it in."

Julie cast a sidelong glance in his direction. She asked casually, "What do you think about this car Jawge? Does it handle nice and do you like it?"

He laughed, "You've spoiled me now, Julie, I won't be happy until I can have one. It's remarkable how it performs, compared to my old jalopy."

Julie looked out her window and smiled. If he hadn't been so stubborn headed, about buying a car and a few other petty things, she would never have done the things she did. Too late now, she couldn't undo the things she'd done, and she wouldn't want to, she assured herself. Men were such fools sometimes. He didn't know when he was well off, or maybe he did, but he didn't appreciate it enough. Sarah's heart ached at the sight of the lonely little house waiting for its loving family to come back to it. "I didn't realize how much I missed it," she thought. She was silent as George drove into the driveway and turned off the engine.

"This is it, darling, my little old port in the storm." George got out and came around to her door.

Julie looked curiously at the pretty red brick bungalow. "Why it's not so little, Jawge. And it's adorable, such a beautiful lawn and shrubbery." Julie stood still and admired the scene. "I'd love to have a sweet little home like this to come back to."

George went ahead and unlocked the door, he glanced quickly to the right and then to the left. What if the neighbors saw them? He hoped they were all busy. Julie went ahead into the living room. George shut the door and locked it.

Sarah warned Julie, "Watch your step, girl. Remember you're a stranger in your own home." Julie smiled lovingly at the familiar surroundings. She turned to George and remarked, "Oh, this is just what I would choose for a cozy homelife." Her gaze traveled around the room. "Just charming. Did you or Sarah furnish it?" she asked so innocently.

"H-m-m-p, I guess Sarah sort of planned it for me. You know how sisters are, especially if they live with you," George confided to Julie. "So bossy and know it all."

"Oh I wouldn't think Sarah would be like that, she's so sweet and docile looking." She was holding her picture, "This is Sarah, isn't it?" George nodded. Julie gasped and ran over to the piano and picked up the picture of Helen. "And this has to be Helen. Isn't she adorable. Oh-h-h, she will look grand in that short coat. You described her so well, I just knew she would look like this Jawge." But George wasn't listening, his mind was on other things. His eyes were hungry, he declared softly . . . "I'm going to kiss you, Julie." He did, thoroughly. "M-m-m, this is better than going riding. Let's kiss some more darling." He took her in his arms and kissed her long and passionately.

"Jawge, you better run along and leave me alone—quick." Julie backed away from him and pretended to be afraid of him. Sarah laughed silently, "Why don't you lead him on and see just how far he would go," but Julie said, "Not yet my girl, I'm not

148

quite ready." George took a short step in her direction, daring her. Julie screamed, and sat down at the piano. "You'll have to take the piano, if you take me Jawge." She glanced teasingly over her shoulder.

"No need, darling, I'm not that much of a wolf. I'll settle for a song." So as Julie's fingers wandered over the keys, George went into his room. Julie sang softly, sweetly to the tempting melody of "Jezebel".

In no time George was back carrying his boots, "Oh-h-h, honey, that can really do things to me," he warned her. He grunted as he pulled his boots on. "Can't remember when I've had this outfit on last. Don't have anyone to go riding with me."

Julie jumped up and came to his side, "Well, I like that, you've got me."

"I mean before you came along."

"Come on George, I want to see the rest of the house and the backyard. You said Sarah had a rose garden for a hobby." Julie strolled towards the kitchen. She stood at the door and admired the gleaming white electric appliances. "Gee I would love to cook in this kitchen."

"H-m-m-p, didn't know you could cook, Julie. Velvet is a swell cook. Sarah's a wonderful cook too, but that maid of ours, Dora, is awful. You don't look like you've ever fried an egg, darling." George bit her pink ear.

Sarah giggled, Julie tilted her head back and looked at George's red doubting face. "M-m-m, you'd be surprised, Mister." And would he.

She dutifully followed him back to the bedrooms and peeked in. Then he took her out to the rose garden. Julie admired and asked questions; Sarah worried and wondered. Would her little plants freeze before she came back? There were several things she had forgotten to take care of. Julie pushed Sarah's harrying thoughts into the background, and listened to George.

" 'Course Sarah does a lot of the work out here, but I have a yard man. No sister of mine is going to be a slave in my home."

Sarah glared at him, but Julie answered sweetly, "Oh-h-h, you

149

must be a wonderful brother and uncle, Jawge. I envy Sarah and Helen having you all the time." She walked back to the house, her arm tucked in his, "Jawge, do you think Sarah and Helen will like me?" She felt his arm tighten.

George coughed, "H-m-m-p, never give it much thought, but why not?" He laughed trying to appear nonchalant.

Julie's long narrow eyes held a wicked look. "I'll bet he's been wracking his brain how to kill me off. Boy have I got him over a barrel. I'll make him sweat blood before it's all over. He won't look at another pretty female as long as he lives." Sarah was silently triumphant.

Julie drove out to the stables, gaily, a trifle too fast for George, but she did it just for a change from Sarah's conservative way of traveling.

At the stables, she asked for Raja. "The finest and fastest horse in the stables," Julie told George. She had ridden Raja many times with Sam trailing along on some "other nag," as he called them.

George chose a fine bay horse that demanded his best display of horsemanship. He admired Julie's grace in the saddle and as they rushed through the wind he had to give way to her supremacy on a horse. "What a woman, there isn't anything she can't do," he told the bay. "I only wish I could turn the clock back about twenty years, and start all over again."

Back at the hotel Julie and George lingered in front of her apartment door. "Please go up and rest Jawge, and go with me tonight out to the Club. They have grand food. Please sugar."

So George promised to go. Julie rushed into the apartment, throwing her hat, coat and riding crop to Velvet, "Get my bath ready, Velvet. I've got to make a couple of phone calls."

She called Tom Masters, "There'll be four at our table, Tom. I'm bringing a guest, Mr. Davis. I want you to see he gets plenty to drink, and take your camera, but keep it out of sight. Sometime during the evening when we're dancing, or sitting very close together be sure and take a picture. I may have to use them, and I'll need some strong evidence. Do you understand, Tom?"

150

"Perfectly. I'll take care of your sugar daddy, never fear."

Next she called Jim Fellows, and her conversation was practically the same as she told Tom Masters. "And Jim, be especially nice to Mr. Davis and see that he gets enough liquor. I want him to enjoy himself."

George came down all decked out in his top hat and tails. He had a heavy top coat draped over his arm. Julie came strolling out of her room, dressed to kill the fatted calf. She wore a creamy chiffon, with jeweled straps, feathers on the full skirt. She wore diamonds on her ears, in her hair, neck, arms and hands. George's eyes couldn't stand the glittering image in front of him. His hand went up to shield his gaze, "Wow, Julie, is it safe to go out there with you?"

"Why yes, Jawge, why?" she asked innocently.

"With all those diamonds on. You should have a guard. One with a gun," he advised solemnly.

"I do have a body guard, Jawge, Tom Masters, but he will meet us at the club. I'll wear my ermine, no one will see my jewels. Don't be afraid, Jawge." Julie smiled sweetly at his worried face.

"Oh, it's not on my account, but yours, dear."

Sarah sneered politely, "Oh yes on my account George, dear old careful, George. I'm surprised you've taken as many chances as you have."

Julie took him by the arm and steered him out the door. "Don't worry sugar, I've got a gun in my bag. I'll take care of you."

George drove the Buick out and cautioned Julie to lock the doors. "It's better to be safe than sorry." He bent over and carefully kissed her perfect lips. "I'm so crazy about you—I couldn't bear to have anything happen to you darling."

Sarah reminded Julie, "I've still got to hear him say he loves you." Julie smiled to herself and mentally promised, "Okay, old girl, before the night's over, I'll have him on bended knees."

The club was a beautifully appointed place. Modern, tastefully furnished, good orchestra, the best floor show in town, the finest food on the northside, and Miss Julie Le Dere. She was packing them in. The Navy was there in force, some with girls and some stag. The place was crowded when Julie and George made their way to the table near the dance floor. A spotlight played on Julie all the way. Whistles, calls, yells and applause, brought waves, bows and kisses from the beautiful Julie. George smiled, smirked and struggled along after her. He tried to ignore the cat calls, the smart remarks and the boos that greeted his appearance. His face was red, and inside he was deeply resentful, but he played his part of Julie's escort beautifully.

She patted his arm after they were seated and fed his abused ego. "You're the most distinguished, most handsome man here tonight. I'm wild about you, Jawge." Her lips formed a silent kiss.

Tom and Jim strolled up to the table and Julie introduced them to George. Tom ordered drinks and Julie barely touched hers. The music started and George asked her to dance, then Tom, and then Jim. Then it was time for Julie to sing. The spotlight followed her all the way to the piano, then it lingered over her shimmering figure. The noise was deafening. Julie stood up and held out her hand, "Please boys, don't you want to hear little Julie sing?" She pouted at the sea of faces.

After they had quieted down she began, she sang "Cold, Cold Heart" twice, then they wouldn't let her go, so she sang, "Sin." The Navy swarmed towards her, "Give me your autograph, you beautiful creature." "Let me hold your hand you gorgeous thing," and so on. Julie signed autographs, held hands, talked and smiled at the lonely sailor boys that hemmed her in.

Back at the table Tom and Jim were plying poor old George with whiskey highballs and he was getting rather out of hand. It took both of them to persuade him to wait for Julie at the table, "Let me get her, those young punks, can't keep my Julie. Let me go." Jim put pressure on one arm and Tom on the other. "I can lick the whole bunch of them. The whole fleet if I have to," he bragged to the two men.

Julie finally made her way back to them, and George was

slightly insulted that she had neglected him. "Oh, Jawge, I'm so sorry, but I have to be nice to my public. Did mean old Julie stay away too long?" Her hand slid up and down his arm.

George tried to focus his pale brown eyes on her smiling face, "Yhes, you don't haf' to make love to the whole Navy." He shook a wavering finger in her face.

"Okay sugar, Julie won't go away and leave you anymore." She winked at Tom. George blinked as the flashlight bulb went off, but he was too wrapped up in Julie to notice what Tom was doing.

Julie listened to George's drunken singsong voice until it was time to sing again. She gently removed his arm from her shoulder. George slumped over the table and tried to talk to Jim. "Jim, old Pal, how about pouring me another drink?"

"I think you've got enough for a while. How about some black coffee?" He motioned to the waiter and soon George was trying to swallow some of the hot liquid.

"It's too hot. Pour some whiskey in it to cool it off," he told Tom.

"You'd better drink it, George, Julie doesn't like drunks," Jim warned the older man.

George's mouth took on an ugly twist, "Who's drunk? Are you? Nobody's going to call me drunk and get away with it." He picked up a coke bottle and swung it around his head.

Jim and Tom both made a grab for him at the same time. Jim wrested the bottle out of George's hand. The two men looked at each other over George's head. "Dame's are sure funny, wasting their time on such tripe."

Jim grunted his disapproval—looking at George's overstuffed figure weaving back and forth in the chair. "I don't get the set up, do you?"

"I have a faint idea, Pal. Sad—how some good looking broads go for these fat old papas just because they have a bank account."

George leered at them, "I heard you, you're just jealous you aren't her sugar daddy." He stood up and pounded his chest.

153

"I am. I'm the King bee. Listen to my baby. Sing Julie, sing." He listened to Julie's voice, she was singing, "You Made Me Love You". When she got to the part where she cried, "Gimme, gimme, what I cry for . . ." George hollered out, "Anything your little heart wants, Julie." He broke from the two at the table and made his way towards her. He stumbled and fell into tables. Julie saw him coming. She bowed—threw kisses left and right as she tried to hurry towards George. "Oh what is the matter with him. Why didn't he stay at the table. He's making a fool of himself—and me too."

George would have made it, if a sailor hadn't accidentally stuck his foot in the way. George fell and hit the table and everything crashed to the floor. Julie stopped in her tracks, and gave a wild signal to Tom and Jim.

Jim grabbed Julie's bag and coat and made for the rear door. George was crawling on the floor, bottles were flying, tables were being upset, women were screaming. One sailor can start a riot and that's just what happened. Somebody hit the sailor and the whole fleet hit back.

Julie was dodging flying objects and urging George to get up, "Jawge, here I am, get up—get up—quick. We've got to get out of here fast." She reached down and grabbed his arm. Just then a bottle whizzed past Julie's silver head, and barely nicked her, but she toppled into George's waiting arms.

"Oh my God, Julie are you hurt. Speak to me darling." George was standing in the center of the melee begging Julie to open her eyes. Tom rushed up and herded George towards the back.

"Get out of here, cops." Then he rushed ahead and when George came towards him—with Julie clutched in his arms, he snapped a picture that would hang him.

They reached the Buick just as the cops roared up to the front. "Jump in, let's get out of here." Jim had the car purring. Tom got in the front and George and Julie in the back. George held Julie all the way home with the ermine tucked around her shapely body.

George murmured sweet endearments in her pink ears. Julie sighed and enjoyed it. She never knew George had it in him. Some day she'd have to tell him of his hidden talents. Maybe he just needed the right woman to draw him out. As they neared the hotel, she opened her eyes and sat up.

"Oh my head, what happened Jawge?" She waved her long lashes at him.

"Oh my poor little girl, my beautiful baby, some old sailor hit you with a bottle. Does it hurt very much?" He was so concerned, so very gentle with his kisses.

Chapter 19

THE NEXT MORNING WAS SUNDAY AND JULIE STAYED IN BED UNTIL noon. She had to laugh at George's worried face, his abject apologies. "Oh my darling, I'm so sorry. Do you think I've spoiled your job?" He held his head and sighed, "I just can't explain it Julie, I never drank more than one drink a day in my whole life, and suddenly I'm transformed into a drunkard. Shameful. The papers are full of the riot. Your name, pictures, and insinuating remarks."

Julie patted his arm and tried to soothe him. "Oh it will be all right Jawge. It won't hurt my job, in fact this will make it even better. The pictures weren't very plain, no one can tell they were you." She smiled into his drawn face. "And the remarks weren't so bad. Merely saying that the gorgeous Julie was rescued from the mob, by a very influential business man."

"Yes, and that he bought her a Buick and was her constant escort and what were his intentions and so on and on."

"Well, what's so bad about that? It's the truth, isn't it?"

George strode over to the cupboard and poured himself a drink. "I better not go out there with you any more, dear, it's too dangerous. I might do something to really get you hurt."

Julie giggled. Inside Sarah said, "M-m-m, what you mean George, is that you might get hurt." Out loud Julie said matter-of-factly, "Whenever there's drinking Jawge, anyone can get hurt.

156

If you prefer not to go it's all right darlin', Tom and Jim will go with me."

"I'd prefer you not to sing in such places. But of course, I don't have the right to dictate to you."

"Oh but you'd love to have the right, wouldn't you, George?" Sarah mentally asked. "You dictated to Sarah for twenty years, but not to Julie, my boy!" Julie laughed, "Now Jawge, you're making noises like a husband."

He walked over to her and sat down. "I wish I were." He slipped his arm around her waist. "Oh, let's forget last night." He held her close and their lips met. "I usually forget everything when I'm with you."

Monday morning Helen called her Daddy at her Mother's detailed instructions. During the course of the conversation, she said, "Daddy, Mrs. Sangster wrote to Mother and told her that she saw you with some show girl. Is that true?" George sputtered and coughed, and of course denied such nonsense, thinking all the time about the Sunday paper. Oh he'd hoped Mrs. Sangster left town or something. Helen went on, "Well, don't forget Daddy, if you ever hurt Mother I'll never forgive you."

Later Helen called her Mother back and related the whole story. She said giggling, "I'd give a lot to know just what does go on down there."

During the week Julie and George went out to the lonely little house, and trimmed the tree George had delivered there. "Julie, I'll get up on the ladder and you hand me the ornaments."

"My this is so different from the last twenty years, I usually had to trim it all by myself and crawl up and down the ladder for hours," Sarah mentally reminded Julie. Each time George came down the ladder which was often, he'd reach over and steal a kiss. "Oh Jawge, you're so sweet. I never knew you were so affectionate." "Neither did I," Sarah told her.

George smirked, and answered softly, "M-m-m, this is just a sample baby." His tone sounded so suggestive.

"We better hurry, Jawge, I have to go to the Radio Studio soon." "Coward why don't you egg him on," Sarah sneered.

157

"That's the only safe job you've got. No artist pawing over you, no Navy to fight off. Why don't you just get two or three broadcasting jobs?" George was tying the big star on the top. "There—is it okay?"

"Fine. It's all done. Let's get going." She began to gather up the boxes and string laying around. "Here sugar, you know where to put this." Julie found her coat and repaired her face, George had kissed all the lipstick off. "He must have a pound of this stuff in his stomach!" she told herself. Sarah quipped, "I wonder how many more flavors he's sampled."

Christmas eve fell on Thursday. Julie called Helen and told her to take the morning train Thursday, which would get her in Chicago, about five P.M. "I'll have my maid Velvet meet you dear, as I will be busy, but she'll bring you to the hotel, and I'll have dinner with you, baby."

Wednesday evening Julie invited George down for dinner. Then she made him highballs, one stronger than the other. Tom Masters was to bring his camera and drop in later.

About midnight, he knocked on Julie's door. George was just about out. "Oh I'm so glad you dropped in Tom. I want you to help me get Mr. Davis up to his room."

Tom and Julie managed to get George to the elevator and then they waited until an empty car came up and they piled him on it. "Whee, I didn't know a drunk could be so heavy," Tom complained.

In George's room, Tom undressed him and put him to bed. Then Julie slipped her coat off and under it she had worn a thin revealing gown. "Now I'll get in here beside this sleeping whiskey bottle, and you take our picture," Julie instructed him. She crawled in beside George and put his arm around her, turned his face to the camera and then she lay close and put her lips against his face so it would look as though he was making love to her. "Now, I think this will do, Tom. Shoot."

Tom hesitated, "Are you sure this is legal?"

"I'll explain it all to you, Tom, and you can see how legal and how fantastic it all is."

158

Tom shrugged, "Well the boss said it was okay, so here goes." He aimed the camera and took two pictures so he was sure one of them was good. "Is that all?"

"That's all, Tom, and you've been a dear. Doing silly things and no questions asked. Do you suppose 'Lover Boy' will be all right if we leave him alone?" She tucked the covers around George and opened the window slightly. It was bitter cold out. She turned out the lights and locked the door. "We'll go down to my apartment. I'll fix you some coffee and tell you a bedtime story."

Velvet came in and out with the coffee, sandwiches and cake, piecing Julie's story as she went. After Julie finished her narrative, she smiled at Tom's perplexed face. "That's about all, Tom, except the grand finale. In the morning, about eight, bring the pictures—all of them—we'll go up and I'll pretend I spent the night with him. You be my witness. I'll have the pictures and we'll see what we shall see."

Velvet clapped her hands silently, her black face beamed, as she whispered, "Oh my, oh my, that I'd like to see, too."

Morning came, Julie slipped out of bed and bathed. "Velvet I'm going up to see how Mr. Davis is. I'll dress later."

After a hurried breakfast and instructions for Velvet to bring a tray up later for Mr. Davis, Julie departed.

She let herself in quickly. George was snoring and huffing like a stuffed hog. "Oh my, what a big head he's going to have," she surmised as she noticed the cold sweat on his forehead. "I'm afraid Jawge is going to be a mighty sick boy. I hate to add to his grief, but it's now or never."

Julie turned the heat on and made herself comfortable in a big chair. "When he decides to start living again, I'll get in bed." She giggled like an eight-year-old, up to something bad.

Fifteen minutes later, a light tap on the door revealed Tom, Julie's companion in crime. "Good morning, how's the beautiful blackmailer this morning?" he whispered at the gorgeous Julie swathed in satin and lace. He admired her with his eyes, then in

159

a hoarse whisper he told her, "My, you look like a bride dressed for her bridal night."

Julie made a face at him, and put her finger to her lips, "Sh-h-h, he'll be coming out of his stupor pretty soon, and I want to be all ready." She motioned to an alcove, where a desk and a lounge chair was hidden from the rest of the big room. "You stay there and listen. I'm going to force a marriage proposal from him. That failing, I'll play the heart broken sweetheart, spurned by her rich lover." She grinned like an imp. "Then you come in and demand fair play for your innocent little client. You can threaten to sue him for trifling with my affections, misrepresenting himself—he's maintained he's a bachelor all along." Julie rocked with glee. "Poor Jawge, I'm a mean widdle kid."

Tom shook his head and took the pictures out of his brief case and spread them on the desk. "What weird things some women can dream up just to prove their point. I hope my wife doesn't go haywire," he laughed as Julie looked at the pictures. "Pretty damning evidence, if I do say so myself," Tom admitted.

"Gee, these are really good and so suggestive. He can't deny them." She put them back on the table. "Don't use them unless we just have to."

"I don't know what possessed a beautiful dame like you to marry an old codger like him, in the first place."

"I haven't always been this pretty Tom, here, I'll show you." She reached in her coat pocket. "This was the Sarah Davis George knew. Now you are looking at the new Sarah Davis, alias Julie Le Dere."

She laughed softly at his baffled expression. He spread his hands out in a gesture of disbelief. "I'd never believe it. I hope you have all the necessary proof to convince him."

"Oh I do, dentist records, all my gold fillings were changed to porcelain, affidavits from Dr. Bloom and Mr. Domere, and a complete report of all the improvements made on my face, figure, personality, habits, and a record of all the lessons I took while I attended the school."

Tom whistled through his teeth, "Whee, all that for him?" He

160

pointed towards the bed. Julie nodded, Tom asked, "Well was it worth it? Are you satisfied and happy, now that you're beautiful, glamorous and talented?"

Julie frowned as she answered his questions, "Naturally I'm happy over my various careers. Don't forget, singing I accomplished as homely old Sarah Davis." Then she sighed, "It's pretty expensive trying to live up to Julie Le Dere, but I've always wanted to be pretty, admired and loved. I guess it was worth it, just so my daughter likes me." Julie peeked in at George, "Still sleeping, like a log. Don't you think it was worth it, Tom?"

He looked at the old Sarah Davis and then at Julie, he grinned, "Yeah, if I thought my old lady could be transformed into a glamour puss like you, I might let her try it. She'd probably leave then." He lit a cigarette and blew smoke rings at the ceiling, "No, I guess I better leave well enough alone." They laughed together, like two conspirators. He tilted his head in George's direction, "I wonder how he's going to like it?"

Julie sighed, "I don't know, it's going to be awfully different. My work, singing, modeling, the public and everything that goes with it. Julie Le Dere as a wife, is going to be a little harder to take than Julie Le Dere, girl friend." Her mouth twisted into a knowing little grin, "But he'll just have to get used to it."

George stirred on the bed. Julie tip-toed in, stood there watching his red bloated face for a few minutes, and then went back to Tom. "I'm going to crawl in beside him now, and wake him up. You'll have to ad lib as we go along. If he suggests money, okay, and if he doesn't, you will. I'm going to hold out for twenty thousand."

Tom asked, "Why that amount?"

"Because that's all the cash he's got in the bank." She winked and walked over to the bed. She threw her coat in a chair, and draped her frothy negligee over the foot of the bed. Then she carefully eased in beside the sleeping George. She propped herself up and yawned, called his name sleepily, "Oh Jawge darlin', it's so late why don't you wake up?" She tried desperately to keep her face straight.

George opened one bleary eye and then the other one flew open as he realized he had a bed partner. He mumbled with a dry, thick tongue, "What are you doing here?" He raised up on one elbow, and then sank back with a groan. "Oh-h-h, my head is bursting. Julie please go away. You can't stay here." His hands pressed against his throbbing head. "Please go home," he pleaded.

"Why Jawge how can you talk like that? Last night you begged me not to leave you. You promised to marry me this morning," she reminded him. George tried to look at her, his face horror stricken. "I did what?"

"To marry me. You begged me not to leave you, and that we'd get married the first thing in the morning. Jawge, what's the matter, don't you love me now?" Julie's beautiful face clouded up.

" 'Course I love you, but I can't marry you. I must have been crazy, or drunk as a hoot owl." He moaned and groaned, "Oh just let me die in peace, please, Julie go away."

"No Jawge, you can't do this to me, you promised to marry me. I've got a witness. Why can't you marry me?" She leaned over him, the frills on her gown tickled his nose.

He reached up to brush them away and his hand brushed against her tear stained cheeks. He opened his eyes and looked at her, "Did I really promise you that Julie?" She nodded her head. "Oh, I'm a heel, a lousy liar. Julie, I'm a married man." Julie let out a loud gasp. "Yes, I'm married. Sarah is my wife, not my sister. Helen is my daughter. Oh I'm sorry Julie. I wish it could be different, but I can't change it, even if I wanted to. You'll just have to forget me." He rubbed his hand over his hot red face. "Oh I never meant to let it get so out of hand."

"But you did Jawge, you spent all your time with me. You led me on, making me believe your intentions were honorable, that you were a bachelor. I can't let you ruin my reputation by just throwing me over like an old shoe." Julie covered her face and sobbed hard. "And I love you more than you'll ever know, oh, Jawge, you're breaking my heart. I won't give you up," she declared.

George groaned and moaned. His big hand reached out and patted her soft arm gently, "I'm afraid you'll just have to, Julie, there's nothing I can do about it." He grimaced with pain.

A voice penetrated his aching skull with cold, cruel words, "Oh yes there's something you can do about it, Mr. Davis. We still have some justice in this cold, cruel world, for poor little girls like my client, Miss Le Dere. We'll sue you, for alienation of affections, and misrepresentation of your marital status. We'll throw the book at you," Tom threatened.

George cried out, "This is a frame-up. You're trying to blackmail me. Okay what proof do you have?" He propped himself up with the pillows.

Julie sobbed, "Oh I don't want money, I want my Jawgie. I love you, sugar."

Tom growled, "Be still Julie. It's pretty evident, 'Jawgie' doesn't want you, so he'll have to pay through the nose." He handed the pictures to George, "Here's enough proof to hang you. Feast your bleary eyes on these. Don't bother to tear them up, I have several of each," Tom warned.

George looked at each one closely, "H-m-m-p, so you had this in mind all along," he accused them.

"No, just merely being careful. A matter of routine. You see, I'm not only Miss Julie's bodyguard and local agent, but also a detective." He flashed his badge.

Poor old George sank down beaten, he waved his hands and moaned, "Okay, you've got me over a barrel. Will ten thousand do?"

Julie looked at Tom, she shook her head. Tom sighed, "Sorry not enough, say twenty thousand and we'll drop all charges."

"Why that's—that's too much. I'll go to court. I'll fight tooth and nail." George beat the bed with his fists.

"Okay, then we'll go to court. I wonder how your wife and daughter are going to take all this." He thumbed through the pictures, "Here is their beloved Daddy and husband, carrying the gorgeous Julie out of the night club, here they are kissing in bed, here——" Tom stopped as George screamed, "Oh-h-h, shut up. Twenty thousand, I'll send you a check," he promised.

Tom's voice was rough as he snarled, "Oh no you don't you old fox, you're going to the bank with us just as soon as you can get dressed," Tom ordered. "Julie you go down and get some clothes on and we'll get this over with," he winked at her.

She slid off the bed, grabbed up her coat and made for the door. Tom added, "Don't worry about Romeo here, I've got a nice little persuader in my pocket."

Julie ran back to Tom, "Oh please don't hurt him, Tom, I really do love my Jawgie." She went crying to the door, "I can't understand——"

"Poor kid, you've just about wrecked her life, you old wolf. I'm glad there's a law that protects these beautiful dames that fall for some old Bluebeard's line. I hope this will be a lesson to you, and you won't try it again." Tom was enjoying himself immensely, as he watched poor old George struggle into some clothes.

The beads of perspiration dripped down George's mottled face. Every now and then he stopped and held his head. "Oh, must I go now?" he appealed to Tom.

"Yes and don't try to pull any funny business in the bank, because I'll be right behind you and the rod you feel in your back won't be a fountain pen." Tom took his gun out and checked the clip.

George shuddered, "Oh why didn't I mind my own business? Why didn't I lock myself up at home? What will Sarah say, no money in the bank. Oh what if Helen finds out. Oh-h-h God."

Tom growled, "Hurry up, Julie will be back any minute and we want to get going."

At that moment, Julie knocked. Behind her came Velvet, with a tray. Hot black coffee, Alka-Seltzer, tomato juice. She set the tray down on the dresser and asked, "Will that be all, Miss Julie?"

"Yes, Velvet. I'll be back for lunch. I have some shopping to do this morning. You may go. Thank you dear." She smiled at her as she closed the door.

Julie appealed to Tom, "Please Tom, let Jawge have some coffee, before we go." She carried the tray over to George, "Here's some hot coffee Jawge, please drink it." She smiled at his old, drawn face.

"Thanks but I think I'll try the Alka-Seltzer, if you don't mind." His hand shook as he picked up the glass of water.

"How you can wait on that old buzzard, Julie, is more than I can figure out. He's had his fling. Now he's through playing and he wants to pick up his marbles and go home." Tom glared at George. "This is one game he isn't going to win."

Julie smiled sweetly and forgivingly at George, "Oh Jawge isn't so bad, Tom, he didn't mean to hurt little Julie, did you sugar?" She smiled up at him.

George tried to smile back, but the Alka-Seltzer backfired and he choked, sputtered and rushed for the bathroom. Tom walked over and tapped on the door. "Don't pull anything funny 'Jawge.' I'll give you five minutes."

Julie called for her car. That made George wince, "A brand new Buick and twenty thousand dollars. That ought to give her a good start," he moaned to himself.

Tom followed George to the teller's window at the bank. George made out a withdrawal slip for twenty thousand dollars. "Big deal on Mr. Davis, or Christmas present?" the clerk asked in a friendly way.

Tom dug his fingers in George's ribs, George answered as naturally as he could, "Both I guess, Dick. Give it to me in big bills, please."

After George counted the money, he slipped it back in the envelope and with Tom keeping him company, they walked over to where Julie waited.

"Twenty thousand, I hope it balances the books, Julie." He gave her a tired smile, handed her the envelope, tipped his hat and disappeared into the crowd.

Julie made a funny little face at Tom. For a minute he

165

thought she was going to burst into tears, but she didn't. "Poor guy, I really knocked him for a loop. I hope he won't do anything drastic. You better keep an eye on him till he gets out to our house tonight, Tom."

The Loop was teeming with people, everyone was rushing madly from one store to another, doing their last minute shopping. The air was cold and stinging. Flurries of snow hit Julie in the face as she pushed, and was pushed, through the Christmas crowd. One minute she laughed, the next she worried. Poor George, what if he disowned her, after he found out she was really Sarah. Could a man disown his wife? What if he hated her now? He wouldn't want her as Julie, or as Sarah.

With her arms full of packages, Julie walked down Michigan Avenue, to the photographer's studio. The wind nearly swept her away. "Brr, I'll be glad to get back to my own little home in the suburbs." Then she mentally added, "That is if George will let me in."

The artist was in a holiday mood, and the time passed swiftly. A very Merry Christmas, Julie. You won't need to report back until the day after New Year's and then we'll really get down to work." He helped her out and Julie trudged down the avenue until she came to the parking lot, where she had left her car.

Velvet was packing when Julie arrived. "You've got so much to pack, I don't know where to put it all, Miss Julie." She waved her arms around at the clothes piled on the bed and chairs. Stacks of gifts that hadn't been unwrapped, shoes, magazines, music, liquor and so many things she had acquired since she had come.

"Call the clerk and get some large boxes. Then we'll have the bell hop carry them down to the car." Julie dropped all her bundles on the bed. "I've got to wrap these this afternoon, but first I want to eat."

So Velvet dropped everything and went back to the kitchen. Soon Julie was enjoying a small lunch. "You know, Velvet, I can't eat very much, even if I wanted to." She glanced down at

166

her flat tummy, "My stomach must have shrunken up to nothing. I haven't gained a pound since I came here."

Velvet laughed, "If you had kept on drinking highballs, you would have soaked up calories like a blotter."

"It's funny how liquor has so many calories and yet is not a food." Julie stared at Velvet. "Do you drink?" She had never seen Velvet indulge or smell it on her breath, but you could never tell.

"No'm, Miss Julie, I learned my lesson a long time ago. I had a good man and I lost him all on account of a bottle." She started to clean off the table.

"M-m-m, I know somebody else who is going to be on rations if he keeps on soaking it up," Julie threatened.

"Yes'm I know who you mean. I think he's learnt his lesson in more ways than one," Velvet giggled as she carried the dishes out. "I'll bet he'll be scared to death of a pretty woman, from now on."

Julie smiled to herself. Maybe he'd be afraid to trust her, too.

After lunch Julie rested, then bathed and dressed for her broadcasting engagement. "Now be sure and meet Miss Helen's train, Velvet. Take her picture and you can't miss her. There's only one little brown humming bird like my girl," Julie smiled. "Gee I've missed her so, this is the first time we've ever been separated. I do hope she likes me." She looked in the mirror. "Do you think she will, Velvet?" Little worry lines appeared on Julie's brow.

"She'll be so proud of you, Miss Julie. 'Course it might take a little time to get used to her beautiful Mama." Velvet was still packing, she stopped, as she asked, "What should I tell her Miss Julie? Don't you think I should sort of prepare her for the pleasant shock?"

"I've been thinking about that Velvet, perhaps you should tell her to expect to be very surprised when she meets me. Tell her I've been completely rebuilt." They laughed happily together. "But be sure to remind her, Velvet, that I'm still the same old Mother inside."

When Julie got ready to go, she called a cab, telling Velvet, "You call a bell boy and have him pack all this stuff in the car. We'll eat here, and then we'll drive out to the house. I'll have to put you in the den until I can arrange something else, Velvet dear." Julie patted the black arm as she passed the maid. "I couldn't breathe without you any more, Velvet."

"That makes me very happy Miss Julie, especially on Christmas eve." She winked back the tears that rushed to her eyes. "This is the first time for a long time, I've had a family, to take care of."

"Well I imagine you know, you've got Mr. Davis spoiled to pieces," she laughed, "and you'll have Miss Helen in the same boat."

Chapter 20

JULIE WAS BREATHLESS AS SHE HURRIED DOWN THE HALL TO HER apartment. She opened the door with her key and walked into an empty room. "M-m-m, guess they didn't arrive as yet." She hung up her coat and noticed that everything had been sent out to the car, and Velvet had tidied the place up. She walked out to the kitchen and looked in the warming oven, "M-m-m, look at that tantalizing meal. Velvet is a jewel, and as long as I can afford to keep her, she's mine."

She went into the bedroom and checked the drawers and closets. All was in order. "I can see where Dora is going to have to watch her step, with Velvet supervising." The phone rang and she answered it quickly, wondering, "Hello?" Then after a short conversation she hung up, a scared little smile playing around her lips. "So George is home, busy as a bee, getting everything ready for his little brown wren and Helen. Oh God, give me strength to face him—and convince him." Julie prayed earnestly. "I've found out so much about him I didn't know, I'm sort of wondering what he might do in a case like this."

Then she heard Velvet's key in the lock. Should she rush out and grab her precious child, or should she wait a few minutes? Julie stood there petrified, Helen's sweet light voice flooding the big room. She was saying, "Oh Velvet, you're a dear, don't worry

169

about me, I'll know my Mother and love her, even if she's painted herself green."

Julie opened her mouth and in her old Sarah Davis voice she called out, "Helen darling, come here."

Helen walked over the soft rugs, laughing, "Oh, Mother, I can't wait—to—" She entered the room and stopped with her lips slightly ajar.

Julie held her arms out, "Don't look so flabbergasted honey, this is your same old Mommy, made over. Don't you like her?" Her lips trembled. Helen rushed into her Mother's arms. They hugged and kissed and then Julie held Helen back and exclaimed, "I do believe Aunt Mary didn't feed you too well, you've lost weight." Sarah's old anxious eyes looked out at the merry brown ones. "Well, tell me how do you like me?" She turned slowly around for Helen's benefit.

The girl took a deep breath and with stars in her eyes declared, "Gee whilikens, Mother, I didn't expect this." She waved her hand. "You look like a Christmas tree angel. Is this what Daddy's been running around with?" Her face crinkled up in a devilish grin. "Wow, I'll bet you had him dancing a tune." Then a shadow crossed her face, "But there isn't one thing that looks like the real you anymore. What did you do? Or maybe I better ask, what didn't you do?"

"Suppose we have our dinner, and while we are eating I'll go into this transformation fully." She linked her arm in Helen's and went back out to the living room, where Velvet had a smoking hot dinner waiting.

Velvet smiled at the two bright faces, "Well Miss Julie, have you convinced her you're her Mother, or does she think you're a new doll Santa's brought her?" They all laughed at Velvet's question.

Helen's eyes strayed back to her Mother's lovely face, "Oh, I believe it's Mother all right, but it's going to take me a little while to get used to living with a glamorous woman every day. The only thing that worries me, is she might steal all my boy friends away from me now."

Julie reached over and squeezed her daughter, "Silly, I'm after the big rich sugar daddys, like your father, poor guy. I've led him a merry chase, Helen. I do hope you and I can convince him to forgive me and take me back." She shook her head and a worried expression filled her eyes, "When I left him this morning, he could have cheerfully shot me."

Helen asked in an innocent voice, "Why, Mother, what could you have done that was that bad?"

Julie laughed gaily, "Well you remember the night we were talking about wrapping someone around someone's finger?" Helen nodded, curious as a little kitten, "I believe this wild scheme of mine was born at that particular moment. Anyway, I wheedled a brand new Buick out of your father, and this morning, he gave me twenty thousand dollars for breaking my heart." Julie stood up and motioned Helen to follow her.

Helen's captivating laughter rang through the room. "Oh, Mother, I'd just loved to have been hiding some place and watched daddy's face. I'll bet he nearly had a stroke parting with all that money. And a new Buick, gosh, that's wonderful, and you said you didn't know how to go about it." The girl's eyes accused her Mother impishly.

"I didn't know then, but it was easy after I had something to work with." Julie dug in her bag, "Come here honey and I'll show you all my proof." She placed the papers in Helen's hands. "Read, and visualize the expense, the misery, the humiliation, the agony I went through to become the famous, beautiful Julie Le Dere."

Helen's brown eyes went over the affidavits and records swiftly, "Isn't it amazing what modern science can do, along with a little human effort?" She giggled at Julie's explosive comment.

"A little human effort, well I like that. If you knew how Lil used to beat me up, and Sam used to ridicule me in front of the class, and make me ride horses that scared me stiff. Oh, Helen, you owe me an apology, my dear." She was only teasing, but Helen kissed the pretty pink cheek and begged:

"Please forgive me, Mother, I do admire your spunk, and I

171

imagine it took a lot of courage for you to accomplish all the wonderful things you do; sing, model. Who said life began at forty? Gee, they were right." Julie reached over and placed her hand over Helen's lips.

"That's one thing we'll never mention again, and that's my age, dear." Julie shrugged, "No one would believe you anyway."

"Okay Mother, you're sweet sixteen from now on. How do the rest of the men like you?"

"Oh-h-h, Helen, at first they scared me to death, I wasn't used to such googey stuff, but now I just ignore it or laugh it off. Here's some clippings you can read some time. All about the fatal beauty, the gorgeous, glamorous, bewitching Julie. It helps my ego." Then she laughed rather sadly, "It's been fun, but Helen, beauty can be a hazard too. I can see now how your poor father must have been tempted more than once by some pretty face. I hope he's cured now." Their eyes met in understanding.

"Talking about daddy when do we see him?" Helen asked her Mother.

"We'll leave right away, as much as I dread it." Then turning to her daughter she asked, "You would never have recognized me would you?" Helen shook her head, Julie went on, "Do you believe me now, that I'm the old Sarah Davis?"

"It's just like you're an entirely different person, except when you talk like you used to, and once in awhile I can feel the sameness about you. Oh, I don't know how to explain it Mother, but I know in my heart you're my real Mother." She dug the rug with her toe, "Gee, do you know I'll have to introduce you to Ham, and all my old friends?"

"Yes and all our old friends, I can just hear George saying, 'This is Julie Le Dere, who is my old wife, Sarah Davis made over.' It's going to be sort of embarrassing for awhile." Julie joined in with Helen's laughter.

On the way out Julie stopped at the desk and paid her bill. Everyone expressed their sorrow at her leaving them. Helen laughed as she remarked, "I just love to hear your southern accent, Mother please keep on talking like that."

172

Julie drove, Helen beside her. Velvet squeezed in the back with all the boxes, "You sure are going home with more than you came with, Miss Julie," Velvet commented.

"You can say that again, in more ways than one." It was fun to whiz along the boulevard in the sleek new car.

Helen examined the dash, felt the upholstery, blew the horn, ohhed and ahhed over the blue Buick. "I'm so glad you finally wrangled this out of Daddy. What are you going to do with our old antique?"

"Sell it, I guess." Driving took all of Julie's skill. She didn't have that false courage without George's critical gaze on her. She could act natural with Helen, she never could drive at night. It was cold and windy, the lake looked angry and sullen in the fading light.

"Isn't Chicago beautiful, Mother? I don't see how anyone can live anywhere else. I'm never going away without you again. I was so homesick, I nearly died. 'Course I would have messed everything up if I'd come back too soon, wouldn't I, Mother?" she giggled.

"I'll say you would." Julie swung into a side street that led to their little bungalow. "M-m-m, the house looks dark, I wonder where he went." Julie parked the car in the driveway. "We'll unload this stuff then I'll take the old bus out and put the new one in."

George had turned the heat up. The house was warm and cozy, the tree lights were burning. "M-m-m, he can't be gone far, probably went to the store." Julie helped bring the boxes and luggage in. Helen took her things in her room. Julie made Velvet welcome and gave her the den as her private sanctuary. "This hide-a-way bed has an inner spring, so I know you'll sleep well. Tomorrow we'll make it more comfortable."

"This is just fine, Miss Julie. I'll be happy here. Don't you worry none about me," the colored woman assured her.

"I'm going into my room. You sort of stay in here, until I've had a chance to see Mr. Davis," she smiled knowingly at Velvet.

"Yes'm, I understand perfectly."

173

Julie was unpacking and arranging the gifts she had brought for the family. She heard George unlock the front door, then Helen's dancing footsteps as she ran to meet her father. Julie listened to the happy excited voices and then she heard George say, "Where's your Mother?"

"I think she's in the bedroom Daddy, unpacking. Boy, are you going to get a surprise for Christmas. The most wonderful surprise of your life." Helen's eyes were bright with secrets.

"H-m-m-p, I hope she didn't spend a lot of money foolishly." He turned to enter the bedroom. Julie hurried and hid behind the door. When George entered she closed it and locked it, putting the key in her pocket.

George had gone straight to the dressing room. Julie called his name softly, "Jawge, dear."

Julie thought she would drop dead, he looked so funny, sort of scared and silly at the same time. He turned slowly to face her. His face worked, but no words came out, then finally he managed a hoarse, "Julie, my God, what are you doing here? Sarah's here—in this house. Go, oh please leave immediately." He had his hands clasped as though he were praying. He closed his eyes and sank on the bed.

Julie tried to keep from laughing, but it just wouldn't stay down and she began to laugh out loud. She walked over and sat down beside George. "Oh Jawge I love you, please don't send me away. Sarah won't mind."

George moved away from her, "Be quiet, it isn't funny." And then a horrible thought came to him, "What have you done to Sarah?" He stared at Julie's smiling face. "Haven't you caused me enough trouble, taking all my money, and now you come here to turn my family away from me." He walked over to the door and tried to open it. "Get out, before I lose my temper." His eyes glared, his face turned red, he was trying to be tough, but he wasn't fooling Julie.

"Oh come here and sit down, and I'll let you in on a little secret. I'm Sarah," she said it in her old voice.

"You're Sarah?" His eyes bulged out slightly, "Now what have

174

you got up your sleeve Julie?" He wasn't trusting her, that was for sure.

"No, honestly, George, I'm you're little brown wren, your very own wife, your old Sarah. Please believe me." Julie put her hand out and touched his arm. "If you'll just sit down here and listen, I'll tell you all about it."

George sat down beside her against his will. "Well, I don't know if you're just crazy or plain nuts, but if Sarah finds us here together I'm going to tell her the truth, and then I'm going to sue you." He reached up and rubbed his head, "My God how much can a man stand." He looked like he had spent a pretty rough day.

"Poor baby, I'm sorry George, you got the worst end of the bargain, but maybe it will turn out all right." Sarah laid all her papers on the bed. She laughed, "Do you remember the night Helen wanted to know how a woman wrapped a man around her finger?" He nodded in a dazed way. "Well that night an idea came to me and I just followed it up." Sarah spread out the affidavits, showed him the records, showed her bank account with the twenty thousand deposited in it that very day. Told him their birthdates, the date they purchased their house, their old gray car and then leaned over and whispered in his ear, "I know your middle name and no one else does." She smiled at his red doubting face.

"Well, it all sounds logical—okay, what is my middle name?" George had never told anyone his middle name but Sarah.

"It is Tucumcari. Your Mother named you after the town in New Mexico where you were born. Now do you believe I'm Sarah?" It would be terrible if he didn't.

"Well, suppose I do believe you. What did you do it for?" He looked anything but happy.

"Oh darling, don't you like me pretty. You were crazy about Julie." She pouted prettily. "I just wanted to be pretty for you."

"I was perfectly happy the way I was, with my nice sweet little wife, and my calm well-run home. Now supposing you are my wife, I'll never have a moment's peace. Men will be pawing all

175

over you, there'll be too much publicity. You'll be either singing, or modeling. I'll be neglected. I'll be jealous. I never had to
worry about my old Sarah." He sighed for the good old days.

Julie sat up straighter, "Well I like that, George Davis. I was
so homely and old-fashioned, you were just too sure of me. Well
the worm has turned, my sweet, I've wheedled a Buick out of
you, I've wrapped you around my finger. I've taken all your
money away from you and now I'm satisfied."

George grinned a sickly grin. "Well, I'm convinced you're still
my Sarah underneath. And I've got a new car, and my money is
still in the family, so I guess I'll have to be satisfied." He looked
at her for a long time and then he suggested, "You better sleep
in the den until I'm more used to you. If I woke up with you in
my bed, I'd think I really was a bigamist." He held out his hand
and drew Julie to him.

"But Jawge don't you like me beautiful?" Sarah's eyes twinkled
as she met his lips.

"M-m-m, I thought if I could just spend the rest of my life
with that gorgeous Julie Le Dere, I'd be in heaven. Now I'm not
so sure. I'll probably be in hell most of the time." He laughed as
he caressed her.

Julie snuggled close, "Silly, I haven't changed inside. And I
had more fun leading you on! But I must say you kept some
things from Sarah. Do you still like Sarah the best?" She didn't
know if she wanted him to or not.

But George wasn't going to be caught in her trap. "I think
I'll wait and see how you turn out, but just between us, I was
awfully fond of the old gal." He kissed the lovely face so close to
his. "This isn't hard to take, though."

Helen pounded on the door, "Come out and talk to your
favorite child. Daddy, how do you like your Christmas doll?"

George laughed as he answered, "Well, it cost me a lot of
money, but I guess it's worth it."

Julie grinned at him, "Yes, sugar, it cost me a lot of money
too."

George reached for the aspirins. "I feel a headache coming

on." He chewed on a couple of pills and looked over at his wife, exclaiming, "This is going to turn into a bigger mess than it already has been. What am I going to tell all our friends and my business associates?" he complained. "I don't know whether to call you Sarah or Julie."

Julie snickered, "Just call me whatever fits your mood, Jawge."

He shrugged his shoulders, "It'll be like living in a fish bowl."

"Oh you'll get used to it, Jawge." She stood up and held out her hand. "Come on, let's go out and join the kids. After all Helen wants to introduce me to Ham."

George groaned and picked up the aspirin bottle. "I was getting along just fine. Why does everything have to get so complicated in my old age."

After Julie had gone out to the kitchen to supervise the mixing of the eggnog, Ham confided to George, "Gee, Mr. Davis, isn't it wonderful, Mrs. Davis discovering all that hidden beauty?"

George moaned and put two more pills in his mouth. "Let me give you some fatherly advice, Ham," he said seriously as he chewed on the aspirin. "Never underestimate a woman."